Nikon D850 User Companion

Your Indispensable Handbook with Illustrations to Master the D850

By

Mats Sauer

Table of Content

INTRODUCTION

The Nikon D850 is a high-end camera that can do a lot of different things. It has a lot of picture detail with 46 megapixels, which is great for photographers who like landscapes and art. It can also take pictures of fast-moving things like sports at up to 9 pictures per second. The camera can take pictures at set time intervals, like watching a flower bloom slowly. It can even make videos that show things changing over time.

If you're wondering how to use this camera, the instruction manual from Nikon could be clearer to understand. Watching DVDs or tutorials online can help, but they don't explain everything well. Who wants to learn about a camera by sitting and watching videos? Wouldn't you rather go outside and take pictures?

The manual that comes with the camera is thick and full of information, but it doesn't explain why you might want to use certain settings or features. It's also poorly organized, so finding what you need is tough. You have to jump back and forth between different parts of the book. The pictures in the manual are not very helpful either.

This user guide is different from other ways to learn about the D850. It uses big, colorful pictures to show you where all the buttons are and what they do. The explanations are longer and more detailed. There's no vague advice like "take a landscape picture" or "take an action picture." Instead, it teaches you how to use every feature of the D850 to take any kind of picture you want. If you need to know where to stand to take a picture of a quarterback throwing a pass, there are other books for that. My book focuses on helping you choose the best settings for different situations, like the right focus mode or shutter speed, to take a great sports picture.

This book is for people who know about Nikon cameras and digital SLRs and beginners who are new to digital photography and SLRs. Both groups of people might feel overwhelmed by all the choices the D850 offers, and they might not understand the explanations in the user's manual. The manuals are good if you already know what you don't know, and you can find answers in a booklet made by someone who works for the camera company.

CHAPTER 1: STARTING YOUR CAMERA

Getting Your Camera Ready to Use

O nce you've taken out your camera and checked it, setting up your Nikon D850 for the first time is quick and simple. You just have to set the time, charge the battery, attach a lens, and put in a memory card. I'll explain these steps individually, but you can skip this part if you already know how to do these things. Even though most people who buy a D850 are experienced photographers, some readers might be new to this, so at the very least, read through the next part a bit. I'll mention a few things you might need to learn about.

Learning About the Buttons and Dials

During this first setup process, you might need to do a few tasks, and many of them will need you to use the MENU button and the multi-selector pad.

- **MENU button:** You'll find this button on the left side of the screen. It's easy to understand; press it to see the menu. To exit most menus or to confirm your choices and leave in some cases, press it again.

- **Multi-selector:** The multi-selector is a button that helps you move around and select things on the camera's screen. It looks like a small button with triangles on top, bottom, left, and right, plus a button in the middle. You can also press it diagonally. You use this button to go through menus on the screen, choose where to focus when taking pictures and switch between different photo details on the screen.

- **Multi-selctor center button:** The center button on the multi-selector is used to choose items on a menu, and you can also press the right directional button for this. The center button can also be used as an OK button, like pressing "Enter," sometimes it can do other things too.

- **OK button:** There's also an OK button on the camera, which I like to use for the Enter function because it's consistent. It can't be changed and usually does the same thing, like confirming actions.

- **Sub-selector:** The sub-selector is another control that can navigate menus, but its main job is to help choose where to focus. You can also press it to lock the focus or exposure.

The main command dial and sub-command dial are located on different camera parts. The main dial changes important settings, like how fast the picture is taken, while the sub-command dial changes other settings, like the opening size that lets in light. For example, in Manual mode, the sub-command dial changes the opening, and the main dial changes the picture speed. You can only adjust these dials when the camera's meter is on, and you might need to wake up the camera by tapping the shutter button.

Touch Screen

The screen on the camera can move around, and you can touch it to do different things. For example, when looking at pictures, you can swipe to see more pictures, tap to zoom in or out, and slide your finger to move the zoomed-in part. You can also use the screen to see small pictures and videos. When you're taking pictures using the screen, you can tap to take a photo without using the button. You can also tap to choose where the camera should focus and even set the camera's white balance by tapping on a specific area.

In Live View mode:

- **Capture images:** While using Live View mode, you can touch the screen to snap a photo without needing to press the shutter button. (Please note that you can't start recording a video by tapping.)

- **Choose where to focus:** Whether you're in Live View or Movie mode, you can designate a focus point by tapping on the touchscreen.

- **Set white balance:** Easily determine white balance by tapping a specific area on the screen for calculation.

In Shooting mode:

Using the touch screen can take time and effort to navigate through menus. The menu buttons and icons on the 3.2-inch screen are small, making it hard to tap accurately. Instead, you can use the MENU and directional buttons to move through menus more quickly.

Enter text: When you need to type text, like entering copyright information in the Setup menu, you can tap the on-screen keyboard to type. It is faster than using the directional buttons to move from one character to another.

You can choose whether to use touch functions or not. You can disable them entirely or enable them only for playback functions (which turns off touch menu navigation). You can also set the direction for full-frame playback "flicks" (left/right or right/left) using the Touch Controls option. Additionally, you can turn off the Touch Shutter/AF feature by tapping an icon on the left side of the screen while using live view or shooting a movie.

When you can make adjustments, a white rectangle will appear around the indicator that can be adjusted using touch. There are triangles for adjusting increments or other icons for different functions.

Here are the available gestures:

- **Flick:** Quickly move one finger from side to side on the screen. During playback, a flick to the right or left goes to the next or previous image.

- **Slide:** Move a single finger across the screen in different directions to scroll around within a zoomed image during playback.

- **Stretch/pinch:** Spread two fingers apart to zoom in on an image during playback, or pinch them together to zoom out.

- **Tap:** Touch the screen with one finger to adjust a menu setting. For example, you can tap triangles to increase or decrease a setting like monitor brightness. During live view, with Touch Shutter activated, tapping the screen focuses on that spot and takes a photo when you lift your finger. If Touch Shutter is off, tapping the screen just moves the focus point.

Because the screen relies on static electricity, it might not work when touched with gloves or fingernails or if covered with a protective film. I have a special glass screen on my D850 monitor, and it works well. However, your experience could be different depending on the cover you use. Avoid using a stylus, pen, or sharp object – use your finger instead. If your fingers are too big, using the physical buttons is better.

Setting the Clock

To set the time on your Nikon D850 camera, you might need to adjust its internal clock to match your local time. If you see a blinking CLOCK indicator on the top screen, that's a sign.

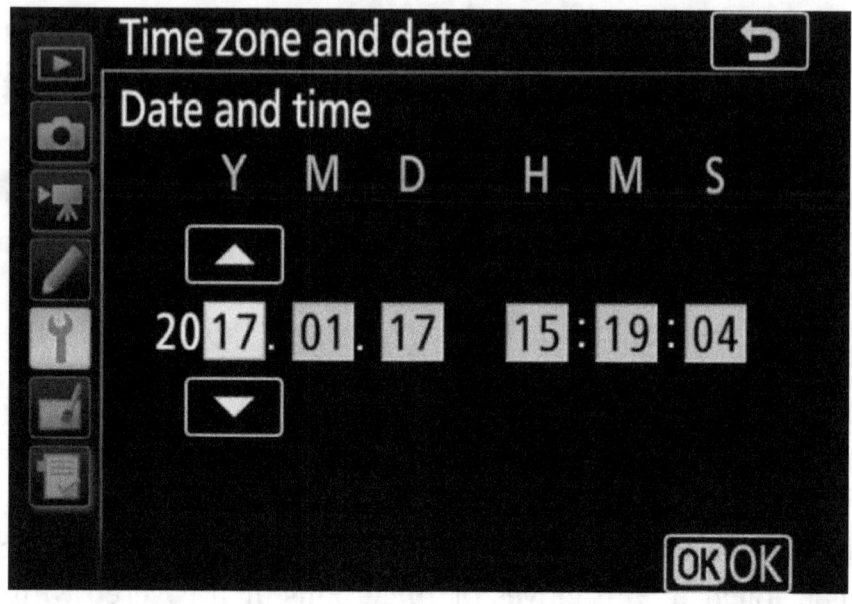

If you're comfortable, you can try this on your own. Press the MENU button, then use the thumb-friendly button (located on the right side of the back screen) to navigate to the Setup menu. Inside, you'll find the Time Zone and Date settings. The camera's clock isn't accurate, so you might need to reset it occasionally.

The clock's settings are saved in a part of the camera's memory powered by a special rechargeable battery. You can't access this battery. If your main battery is low or removed for a long time, this special battery might lose power, causing the clock to forget the time settings. It will recharge when you put in a fresh EN-EL15a battery, but this can take a few days, and you'll need to set the clock again.

Charging the Battery

When you correctly put the battery in the charger, a light blinks. It blinks until another light turns on, which means the battery is fully charged in about 2.5 hours. You can use a cable or a plug adapter to connect the charger to a wall outlet. Once the battery is charged, put it back in the camera. To be sure it's fully charged, check the Battery Info in the Setup menu. If it's not charged, try putting it in the charger again. There are three reasons: a) charging might take longer, b) a new battery needs a few charge cycles to work well, and c) the battery might be broken. The last one is rare, so ensure the battery is charged and ready before relying on it for a certain number of photos.

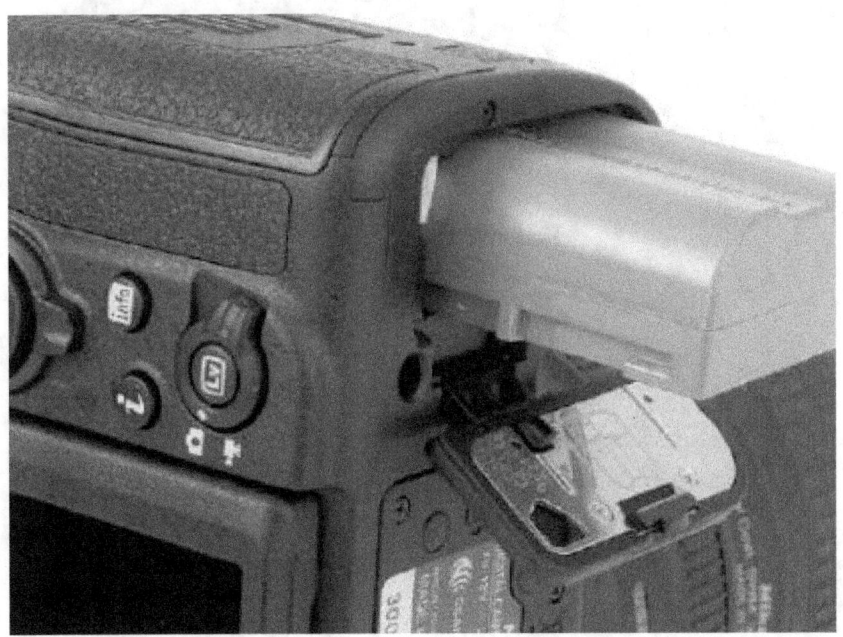

Mounting the Lens

Putting the lens on your camera is important, and I'll explain how to do it safely. First, if your camera doesn't have a lens on it, choose the lens you want and loosen the cap at the back of the lens, but don't remove it completely. Keep the lens ready in your bag where it's safe but easy to reach. Loosening the cap lets you take it off just before attaching the lens, so the back of the lens stays protected.

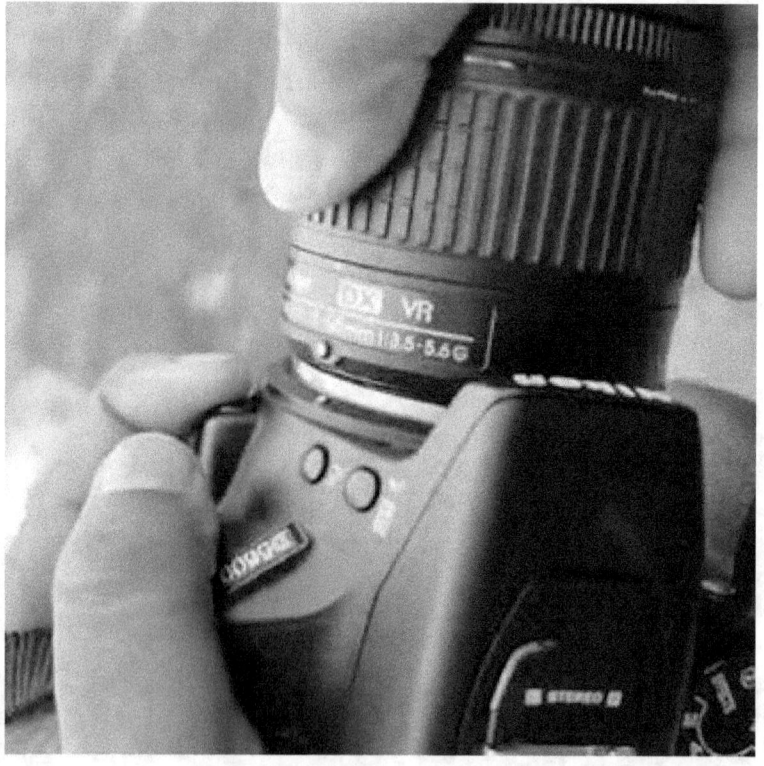

Next, remove the cap from the camera body by turning it away from the release button. Always use this cap when you don't have a lens on the camera. It helps prevent dust from entering the camera and settling on important parts like the mirror, the screen for focusing, and the area around the sensor. Even though the camera has a cleaning mechanism for the sensor, it's best to have as little dust as possible.

Now that the body cap is off remove it from the back of the lens, put it aside, and attach it to the camera. Match the line on the lens with the white bump on the camera where you attach the lens. Turn the lens until it fits securely. Some lenses might be tricky to attach, especially telephoto ones or zoom lenses with parts that move for tripods. You should turn these parts to avoid hitting the camera's front part.

If the lens can focus automatically, set the switch on the lens to "AF" or "M-AF." If the lens hood is attached to the lens but turned around (this makes the lens and hood smaller for carrying), take it off and put it back on the right way, with the curved parts facing outward. The lens hood protects the front of the lens from bumps and also stops extra light from causing glare on the lens.

Adjusting the Diopter

If your eyesight isn't perfect and you wear glasses, you might need help seeing clearly through the camera. If your glasses aren't on, you can adjust the camera's built-in diopter to sharpen the viewfinder. Just pull out and turn the diopter control next to the viewfinder until your subject looks clear. Use a real image, not just the indicators, for accurate focus. Your glasses or contact lenses might be enough to help you see well, but if you wear glasses and want to use the D850 camera without them, you can change the camera's built-in diopter adjustment. This adjustment can be changed from -2 to +1 correction. To do this, pull out the diopter adjustment control next to the viewfinder and then turn it while looking through it. Keep turning until your subject looks sharp. Remember that the focus screen and the indicators outside the image area might seem slightly different, so it's better to use a real image to judge focus accurately.

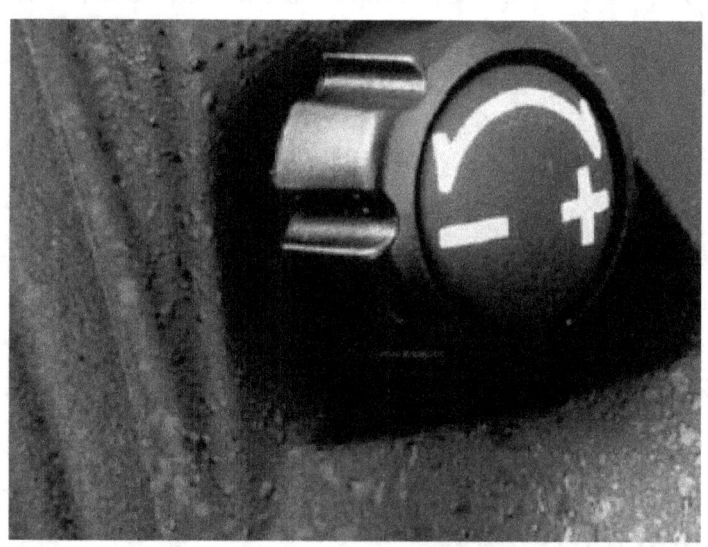

If you wear glasses or contacts but want to use a camera without them, you can adjust the viewfinder to make things look clear. There's a dial near the viewfinder that you can pull out and turn to help you see better. Look through the viewfinder and turn the dial until what you see looks sharp. If more than one person uses the camera and needs different settings, you can remember how many clicks and how you turned the dial. If the adjustment isn't enough, you can buy special lenses for the camera's viewfinder that cost around $16 each to help you see even better.

Inserting a Memory Card

Put a memory card into your camera so you can take photos. Open the small door on the back-right side of the camera, revealing slots where you can insert memory cards. There are two slots: one for SD cards and another for XQD cards. You can use one card or both. The camera will work with just one card inserted.

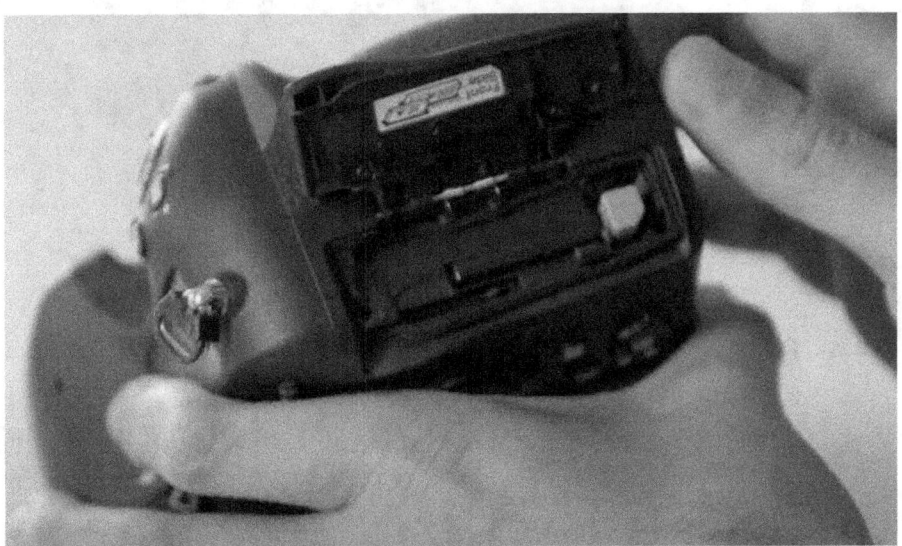

Make sure to put the memory card in with the label facing the back of the camera and the metal contacts going in first. Close the door and format the card if needed. To remove the card, press it in, and it will pop out a bit so you can take it out. Remember to take out the card when the camera is turned off or not writing to it.

Exploring the Buttons and Features on the Camera

Topside Control

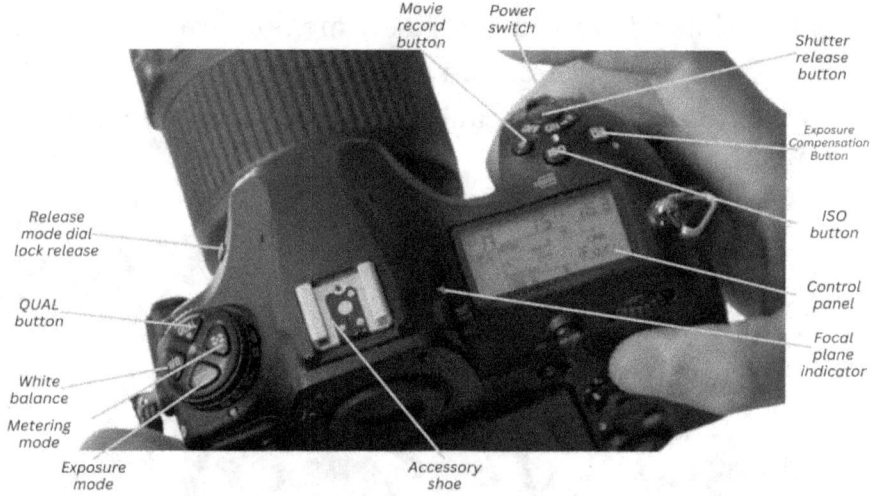

- **QUAL Button:** Change the type of picture quality by turning the dials. You can pick between RAW, JPEG, or TIFF. Adjust the size of JPEG images using another dial.

- **Release Mode Dial Lock Release:** Press to unlock and adjust the Release Mode dial.

- **Release Mode Dial:** Choose how the camera takes pictures.

18

- **Camera Strap Eyelet:** Attach your camera strap here to carry it easily.

- **WB (White Balance) Button:** Change the colors in your pictures by turning the dials. Make them warmer or cooler as needed.

- **MODE Button:** Change how the camera takes pictures by turning the dial. Choose between modes like Auto, Aperture Priority, Shutter Speed Priority, and Manual.

- **Metering Mode Button:** Change how the camera measures light by dialing.

- **Stereo Microphones:** Record sound when making videos.

- **Movie Record Button:** Press to start or stop recording videos.

- **Power Switch:** Ensure to turn the camera either on or off.

- **Shutter Release Button:** Press halfway to focus fully to take a photo.

- **Exposure Compensation Button:** Adjust the brightness of your photos using the dial.

- **ISO Button:** Change the camera's sensitivity to light by turning the dials. You can also turn on or off automatic sensitivity.

- **Control Panel:** Displays various camera settings.

- **Diopter Adjustment Control:** Adjust the viewfinder's focus to match your eyesight.

- **Focal Plane Mark:** Helps measure the distance from the subject to the camera's focal point.

- **Accessory Shoe:** Attach extra accessories like a flash unit.

Front Features

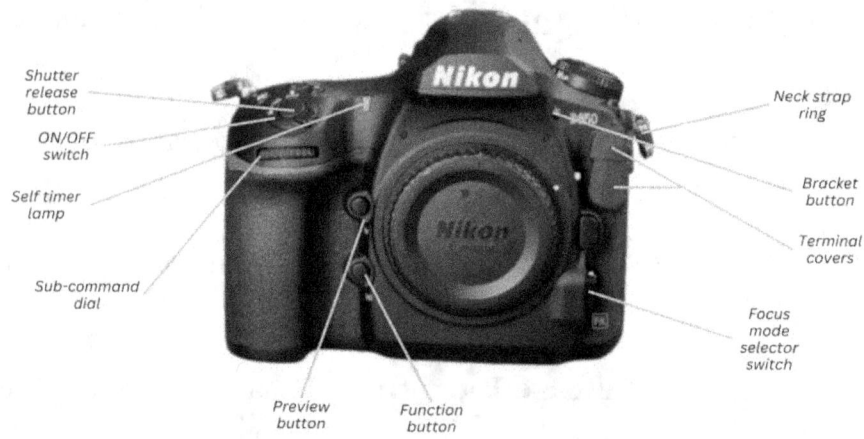

- **Self-timer lamp:** When you set a timer for a photo, a blinking light shows the countdown.

- **Quick return mirror:** This flip-up mirror makes the picture from the lens go up to the screen you look through and the exposure metering system. Then it goes to the eyepiece of the viewfinder. Some mirror parts let light down to the bottom's autofocus system.

- **Auto aperture lever:** A lever that moves the lens inside to the right f/stop for the picture. The camera decides the opening size based on the exposure settings or your choices in certain modes. It uses the metal parts on top of the lens mount to know what you want. Be careful not to damage the lever by putting the lens on the camera at a weird angle. Nikon often has to fix this issue.

- **Electronic contacts:** These points touch the lens mount to talk to the lens. They let the camera and lens share info about the aperture and focusing.

- **Lens bayonet mount:** This mount connects the camera and lens. It has mostly stayed the same since the old Nikon F camera in 1959, except for some updates. It's held on with screws but not too tight. This way, if the camera falls on the lens, the mount might come off instead of damaging the camera badly.

- **Meter coupling lever:** There's a little moving part on the lens ring next to where you attach the lens to the camera. It connects with a notch on lenses that have their aperture control. This part shows the camera how wide the lens can open and the aperture you've chosen.

This helps the D850 work with older lenses without autofocus (like AI or AI-S) in Aperture-priority mode.

You just need to enter the lens details once in the menu and let the camera know when you're using that lens.

Because of this part, for lenses that autofocus and have a "D" in the name, you need to lock the aperture at the smallest opening (like f/16 or f/22) using a switch on the lens. This way, the lens can share its aperture details with the camera. But this doesn't matter for lenses without an aperture ring, like the "G" type.

- **Autofocus drive screw:** For lenses that can't focus by themselves, there's a thing called the autofocus drive screw, which is found in more advanced cameras like the D850. This part helps the camera focus lenses that don't have a special focusing motor in them. The D850 can focus on different types of these lenses, while simpler cameras can only focus on certain types.

- **Lens release button:** The lens release button takes off a lens from the camera. Press this button to unlock the lens, so you can turn it and remove it.

- **Lens release locking pin:** The lens has a pin that goes into a hole to stop the lens from turning. You can release the pin by pressing a button.

- **Power connector cover:** The power connector cover is a little door that you open to plug a cable into the battery compartment to charge the camera.

- **Memory card door:** The memory card door is where you insert your memory cards. You open the door by sliding it towards the back of the camera.

- **Shutter Release:** On the top of the hand grip, there's a slanted button called the shutter release. It does different things depending on how you press it. If you press it halfway, it locks the focus and exposure. Press it down to take a single photo or a bunch of them in a row if you change to the continuous shooting mode. You can also use it for the self-timer to take multiple shots after a delay. If the exposure meters turn off, you can turn them on again by tapping this button. And if there's a menu or a picture on the back screen, tapping this button can make it disappear.

- **On/Off Switch:** Turning this switch to one position turns on the camera. Turning it further illuminates the top screen in dim light for reading settings.

- **Sub-command Dial:** This dial changes camera settings. It works with another dial to adjust the shutter speed and aperture. You can customize its behavior in the camera's settings.

- **Hand Grip:** This part helps you hold the camera and the battery. You don't need to remove the battery to attach accessories like a vertical grip.

- **Function 1 (Fn1) Button:** This button can be programmed to change metering modes or turn off the flash.

- **Preview Button:** This button closes the lens aperture to the chosen setting before taking a photo. You can change its function just like the Fn1 button.

- **Bracket button:** Press and hold this button while turning the main dial to choose how many pictures you want to take with varying settings. Use the other dial to decide how much the settings change between each picture. If you set the number to zero, this feature turns off.

- **Neck strap ring:** There's a little ring attached that you can use to connect a neck strap to the D850 camera.

- **Lens mounting index:** Match the dot on the lens with the dot on the camera to properly attach the lens.

- **Lens autofocus/manual focus switch:** You can switch between automatic focus and manual focus by using this switch on the lens or the one on the camera.

- **Port covers:** Three rubber covers protect the USB, HDMI, microphone, headphone ports, and GPS/accessory terminals when you're not using them.

- **Focus mode selector switch:** Turn this switch between automatic and manual focus. Just remember that the setting on this switch and the one on the lens should be the same. The camera switch should be set to AF if the lens is set to A (or M/A, allowing manual autofocus fine-tuning). If either one is set to M, the lens should be focused manually.

- **Focus mode button:** Press this button and turn the main dial to switch between different autofocus modes or manual focus. Use the other dial to change how the camera selects the focus area.

- **Flash sync terminal (inset):** This is a hidden connector under a cover that you can use to attach things like a flash or other accessories.

- **10-pin remote terminal (inset):** This connector is for accessories like remote control cords, GPS connections, and more.

Back-of-the-body Controls

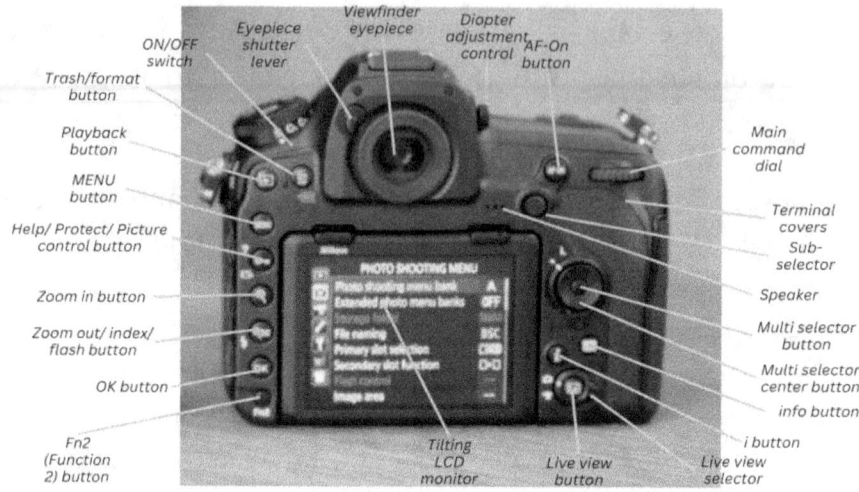

These are the controls at the back of the camera:

- **Viewfinder:** Look through it to frame your photo without using the screen.

- **Eyepiece Shutter Lever:** Close the shutter without using the viewfinder to block light.

- **Trash Button:** Delete the current photo on the screen.

- **Playback Button:** Show the last taken photo on the screen.

- **MENU Button:** Open and close the menu.

- **Image Protect/Picture Control/Menu Information Button:** Press to keep a photo safe / Change picture settings / Get more info.

- **Zoom In Button:** Make the photo on the screen bigger.

- **Zoom Out/Flash Button:** Make the photo on the screen smaller / Adjust flash settings.

- **OK Button:** Pick an option in the menu.

- **Fn2 Button:** Customizable button for specific settings.

- **Tilting Monitor:** The screen can be moved and tilted.

- **Viewfinder Eyepiece:** The rubber piece you can take off when the eyepiece is closed.

- **Speaker:** Makes sound.

- Sub-Selector: Choose where the camera focuses.

- **AF-ON Button:** Use to focus.

- **Main Command Dial:** Adjust camera settings.

- **Multi Selector:** Navigate menus or pick focus points.

- **Focus Selector Lock:** Keeps the focus point from changing.

- **Memory Card Slot Cover:** One slot for XQD cards, one for SD cards.

- **Info Button:** Show or hide info on the screen.

- **Live View Selector:** Switch between photo and video modes.

- **Live View Button:** Start Live View.

- **i Button:** Opens a menu based on the mode you're in.

- **Memory Card Access Lamp:** Lights up when writing data to cards. Don't turn off the camera then.

Working with Memory Cards

There are different ways to empty a memory card for your camera, but only some of them are correct.

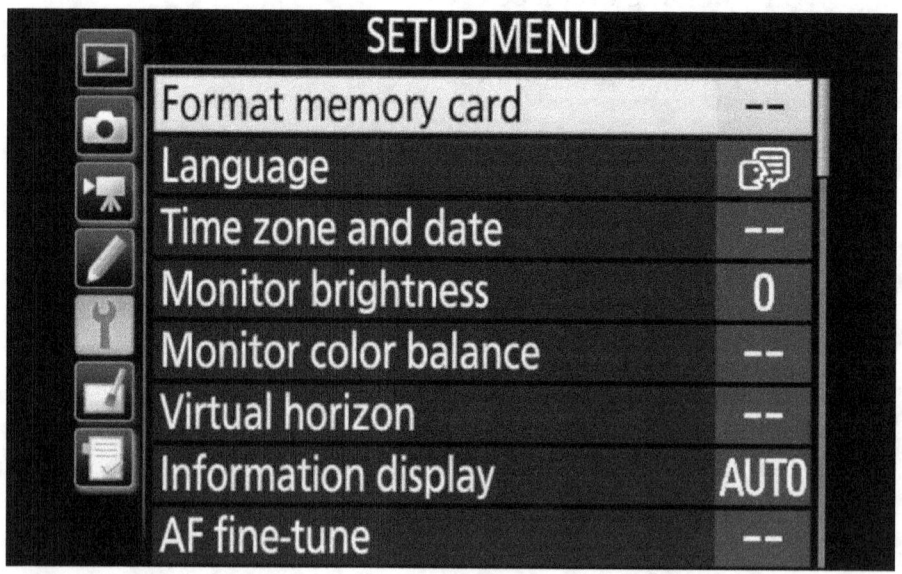

Here are the options you have:

- **Transfer Files to Your Computer:** When you move the image files from your memory card to your computer, the old images will be erased, and the card will become blank. However, this method won't remove protected files or fix corrupted parts of the card.

- **Don't Format on Your Computer:** Avoid formatting the memory card using your computer's software because it might not work correctly for your camera. The best way to ensure the card is correctly formatted is to do it in the camera unless it is seriously damaged.

- **Setup Menu Format:** You can use the camera's menu to format the memory card. Go to the Setup menu (wrench icon), choose "Format Memory Card," select the card type (XQD or SD), and confirm the format. I suggest using the Setup menu format to be safe. It takes longer, but it's better than accidentally erasing all your images. The two-button method is another option, but be careful with it.

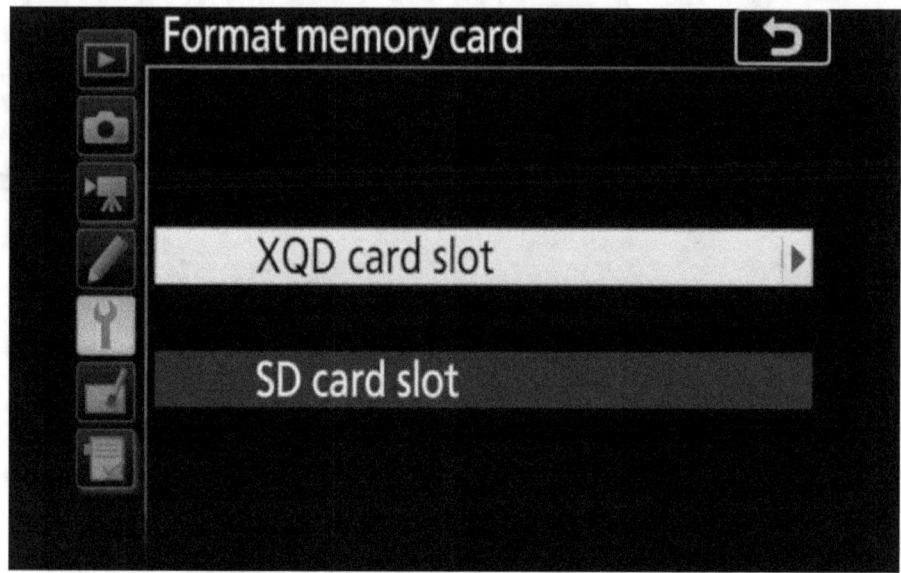

- **Two-Button Format:** Hold down the ISO and trash can buttons simultaneously for about two seconds. The camera will format the primary slot if you have cards in both slots. You can change the slot using the main command dial on the back.

CHAPTER 2: GETTING GOOD AT AUTOFOCUS

Understanding Focus

Before, in the old days of film cameras, people had to focus manually. Even though the viewfinders were bigger and better, photographers still needed special tools to help them focus correctly. Imagine how tough it was to focus well in fast-moving situations like sports photography.

Manual focusing is hard because our eyes and brains don't remember to focus well. It's like when your eye doctor switches lenses during an eye exam and asks, "Which one is easier to understand? Just like that, manual focusing means turning a ring on the lens to get the right focus. You go from almost clear to clear to almost clear again. The little movements get smaller until you find the right focus point. You're looking for the picture with the most contrast between different parts.

Modern cameras, like the Nikon D850, have autofocus systems. They also notice when things get clearer or blurrier, but they remember this process well. So, autofocus can work faster and more accurately with enough contrast in the image. But the camera only sometimes knows for sure what it should focus on. Is it the closest thing? The middle subject? Something behind the closest thing? Someone at the side of the picture? You need to tell the D850 exactly where to focus to use autofocus well.

Learning to use the D850 camera's modern autofocus is simple, but you must understand how it works to get the best results. Once you're comfortable with autofocus, you'll know when to use manual focus. Remember that focus is sometimes different; something that looks sharp at one size and distance might not be sharp at a different size or closer distance.

Getting the best focus can sometimes mean making everything look sharp. Some parts of an image might intentionally need to be more focused for creative reasons. Controlling what's sharp and what's not is part of your creative tools. Using depth-of-field to blur parts of an image while keeping other parts sharp is a valuable skill for photographers. But this works only when the right areas are in focus.

The D850's autofocus, like other SLR cameras, judges focus, but unlike human eyes, it can remember progress perfectly. This helps autofocus lock on faster and more accurately, especially with high-contrast images. However, the D850's focus system can't know what should be the sharpest. Effective autofocus requires you to choose which area the camera should focus on by selecting a focus zone.

The camera uses its sensors to figure out if the picture is clear. It checks if the subject is moving and even tries to guess where it will be when the picture is taken. Autofocus speed is how quickly the camera can do this and adjust the lens to make things sharp. Sometimes, the camera might not be fast enough, like shooting fast sports. In that case, you can switch settings or focus manually.

There are two main ways the camera gets things in focus: one for still pictures and videos and another when you look through the viewfinder. I'll start by explaining the first way, and then I'll talk more about the second way.

Autofocus Mode

This setting decides when your D850 camera starts focusing and what it does once it's focused. The camera doesn't focus all the time to save battery. Normally, it only starts focusing when you press the shutter button halfway.

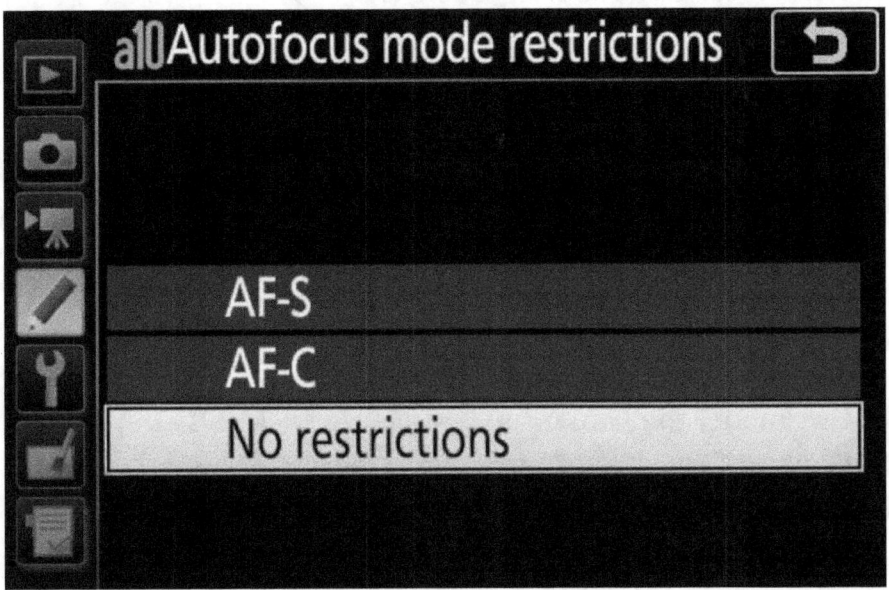

Single-Servo Autofocus (AF-S)

In Single-Servo Autofocus (AF-S) mode, the focus is set once and stays that way until you take a picture or release the shutter button. This mode is good for still photos to avoid blurry shots, but it might make you wait if the camera tries to focus. When the focus is right, the chosen focus point blinks red, and a light at the bottom left glows. If you use Matrix metering, the exposure is locked too. Holding the shutter button halfway lets you change the framing while keeping focus and exposure. You can also use the AE-L/AF-L button if you've set it up. This mode uses less battery and might cause a bit more delay in taking photos.

Continuous-Servo Autofocus (AF-C)

This mode is called AF-C and is great for sports and fast-moving things. When you press the button halfway, the camera focuses and keeps watching the subject. If it or you move, the focus adjusts. The real focus and brightness are set when you press the button to take the picture. AF-C is the fastest autofocus mode, but it uses a lot of battery because it keeps focusing.

In this mode, the camera uses a clever trick called predictive tracking to focus on things moving toward or away from it. It looks at where you want to focus or where it thinks is best in Auto-area AF mode.

If you want the focus to stay the same for many pictures, you can lock it by moving a switch or pressing a button.

Manual Focus

When you turn a switch on your camera's lens to "M" or use a switch on the camera body, you can control your focus on the

D850. You can't use autofocus if both the camera and lens are set to manual focus. This approach has pros and cons. The batteries last longer in manual focus mode, but focusing on each photo takes longer, which can be challenging. Unlike older film cameras, modern digital cameras, including dSLRs, rely heavily on autofocus, and their viewfinders aren't optimized for manual focus. Film cameras have larger, brighter viewfinders with screens that make manual focus easier.

Back Button Focus

After using your camera for a while, you'll come across the terms "back focus" and "back button focus." You might wonder if these are good or bad. They're different from each other. The back focus could be better; it happens when a lens focuses on something behind your intended subject. Some of your lenses might have this issue, while others may not. The good news is if it's just a problem with a lens (not a camera issue affecting all lenses), it can be fixed. How to fix it will be explained later.

On the other hand, back button focus is a tool that lets you separate two usually connected functions: setting exposure and focusing. It can be helpful because you can lock in exposure and then focus separately or vice versa. It's a helpful tool, but using it effectively might require changing habits and learning new ways to use your fingers.

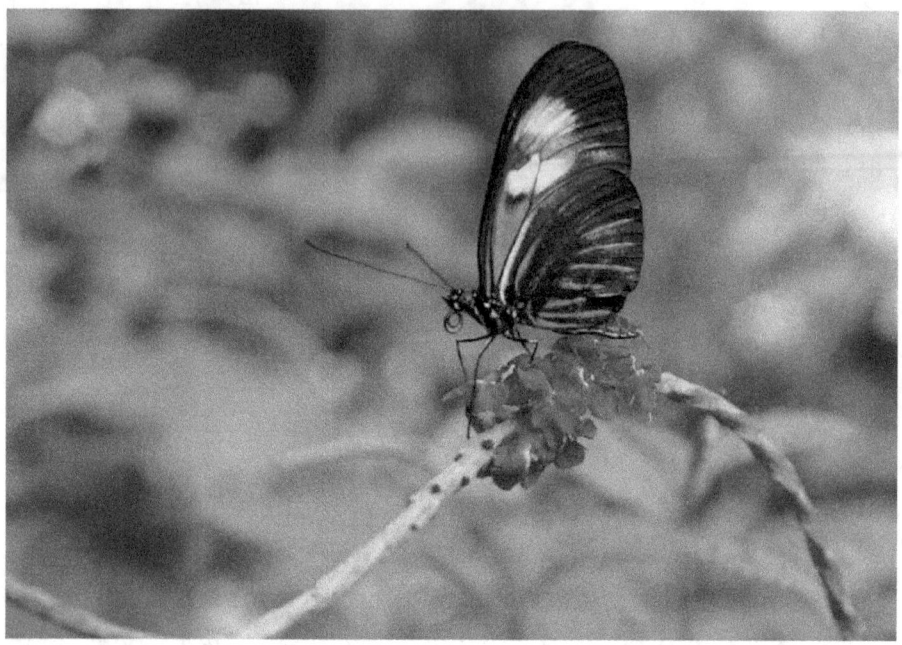

Back button focus is like having a special way to control your camera's autofocus. Instead of autofocus being always on, you can decide when to use it. For example, if you're waiting for a player to come into view at a sports event, you can set the focus where you expect the player to be and only turn on autofocus when the player shows up. With cameras like the D850, you can choose which button to use for this and how it behaves. It might take some practice to get used to as you learn which techniques work best for you.

Back button focus means you don't have to switch between different autofocus modes when your subject starts moving. You're in charge of when autofocus gets activated. It is really helpful for sports photography when you want to focus precisely when the action happens. It works for still photos, too.

You can press your chosen focus button to take several pictures with the same focus, which will only change once you press the button again.

Want to focus on a specific spot that's not part of the camera's regular focus areas? You can use the back button focus to set the focus exactly where you want and then adjust the frame without losing focus. Are you worried about missing important shots, like at a wedding or during a photo assignment? If your camera is set to prioritize focus, it might wait to take a photo until the focus is perfect. With back button focus, you can focus first and take the shot when you're ready, without any delay. It can also help save battery because image stabilization only kicks in when you focus.

Activating Back Button Focus

You can change how the camera's back button works. To do this, go to Custom Setting a8, AF Activation. You can choose between two options: Shutter/AF-ON or AF-ON only.

If you pick the first option, pressing the shutter halfway will set the exposure and focus. The second option, AF-ON, separates these actions. It means focusing starts only when you press a specific button.

Regarding the button itself, you have choices. Most people like the AF-ON button, but you don't have to use it. You can choose a button that's easy to reach and works as you prefer. For example, the Fn1 or Preview buttons (both located near the lens on the camera's front) are options. Custom Setting f1 lets you choose your preferred AF-ON button.

You have different options for how the back button behaves:

- **AE/AF Lock:** Locks both focus and exposure while the button is pressed. It's like how the AE-L/AF-L button worked in earlier cameras.

- **AF Lock only:** Locks focus while the button is held down. Letting go of the button and pressing it again makes the camera refocus.

- **AF-ON:** Pressing the button starts autofocus, and the shutter button can't trigger autofocus. This is the traditional back button focus. You can also set the AF-ON, Fn1, and Pv buttons for other exposure-only actions while leaving AF activation to another button.

- **AE Lock only:** Locks exposure when the button is pressed; more useful if you care about exposure locking more than back button focus. The shutter button can still lock exposure and AF as usual.

- **AE Lock (Hold):** Exposure locks when you press the button and stays locked until you press it again or a timer expires.

Fine-Tuning the Focus of Your Lenses

In this part, I'll show you how to make your camera's lenses work better using a feature called AF Fine-Tune on the D850.

This feature is available on professional camera models like the D850, D5, and D500. The D850 has a lot of detail, so even small focus mistakes can be seen. AF Fine-Tuning can help fix this more on the D850 than cameras with fewer details.

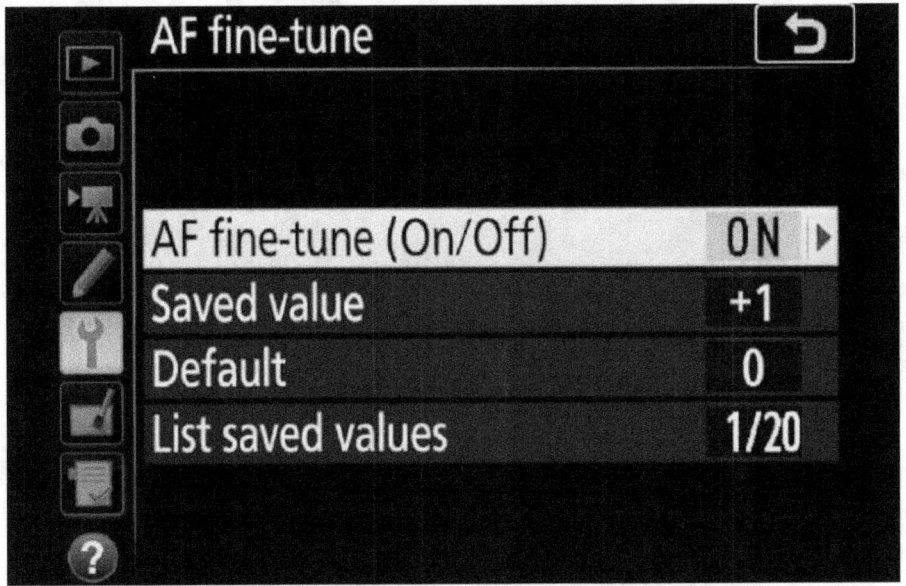

Now, why are some lenses not focusing well in the beginning? There are many reasons, like the lens being old and focusing a bit differently, the effects of temperature and humidity on specific types of glass, and tiny differences in how the lens is made. These factors can cause a slight misalignment, even though the parts are technically okay. Even a tiny difference in how the lens is attached can change the focus slightly. If a lens consistently focuses a bit behind the target, it's called back focus. If it focuses in front of the target, it's called front focus.

If your camera isn't focusing well, you can send it to Nikon to get it repaired. But if that's not possible, like if you didn't buy your lens from an official seller, there's another option. If only a couple of your lenses have focusing issues, you can try fixing them yourself. Here's how: Put graph paper on a flat surface, put an object in the middle, and take a picture at an angle using your lens's widest opening and the autofocus mode you want to test. For accurate results, ensure to use a tripod.

CHAPTER 3: MASTERING COLOR CONTROLS

Understanding the White Balance Setting

I t is like a tool in a camera that helps make sure white things look white and other colors look right, no matter what kind of light you're using. You can also change these settings to add interesting colors to your pictures.

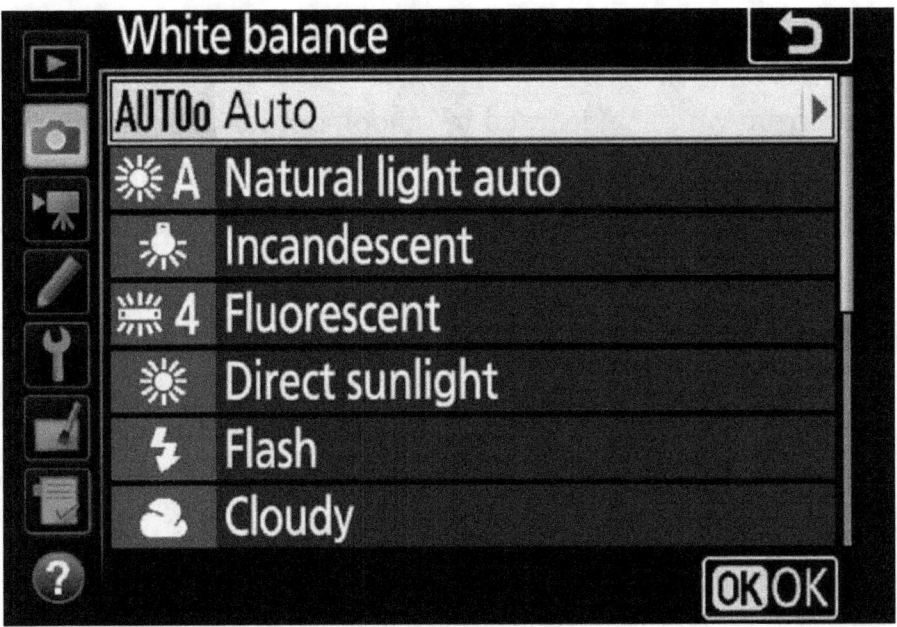

Imagine thinking about colors in a different way than usual. Usually, when we talk about stars, we say that a red star is cool and a blue/white star is hot. But with white balance, it's the opposite. It adds colors to fix what's missing in the original light of the thing you're taking a picture of.

For example, when you're under fluorescent lights, there's not enough blue light, making things look greenish-yellow. By adding blue, the picture looks more normal and balanced.

Think about taking a picture on a cloudy day. The light can make the picture look bluish. To fix this, the camera's White Balance control adds red to warm the colors. The camera's White Balance might be around 6000K on a cloudy day.

Remember, I use the Kelvin temperature range differently. Warm colors are like red, and cool colors are like blue. It might differ from what you learned in school, but for photographers, red is warm, and blue is cool. Don't let your astronomer friends confuse you.

White balance means knowing that light can have different colors, like cool or warm. I can change our camera settings to capture accurate colors depending on the light source. If I don't adjust the settings, the picture might have a colored tint.

Fine-tuning White Balance

You can change how colors look on your camera to make whites appear better. You can do this in two ways: using the Information display or the Shooting Menu. Let's start by looking at the Information display method.

Fine-Tuning With the Information Display

To change the color balance, your camera offers different options. You can add more amber (A) or blue (B) and also more green (G) or magenta (M) by making minor adjustments. You can add or remove amber or blue in steps, like A1 to A6 or B1 to B6, in little steps of 0.5. Similarly, you can add or remove green or magenta in smaller steps like G1 to G6 or M1 to M6, which are even smaller at 0.25 increments. Each complete step changes the color by about five units, half a step changes it by about 2.5 units, and a quarter step changes it by about 1.25 units. You can change up to 30 units for these four colors, like A6.0, B6.0, G6.0, or M6.0. But a slight change of 1 unit might be hard to notice.

Once you change something, like the white balance, you'll see a star () next to it on the Control panel. This star will also appear next to the white balance name on the camera's screen and in the menus. For instance, if you adjust the Shade or AUTO white balance, you'll see Shade or AUTO. The star goes away when you undo the change.

Here's how to make the colors look different in your pictures taken with your Nikon camera:

1. Press the info button once to see the camera information.

2. Hold the WB button and turn the back dial to pick a color setting like AUTO or others.

3. While holding the WB button, press left to make it more yellow, right for more blue, up for more green, and down for more purple.

4. When you're satisfied, let go of the WB button. The color change will be applied to your photos until you adjust it again. Look at your pictures to see if you like the new colors.

Fine-Tuning With the Shooting Menu

You can change the colors in your photos using the Shooting Menu. You can adjust four colors: amber, blue, green, and magenta. If you saved a white balance setting before, you can still change it using the Shooting Menu. You can make the colors more green, amber, magenta, blue, or a mix of these.

Here's how:

1. Navigate to the Shooting Menu and select White Balance.

2. Pick a type like Direct Sunlight. You can adjust it by moving right or pressing OK to keep the current setting. If you want to adjust, you'll see a colored box with a black square. Black means no change. Press up for more green, down for more magenta, left for more blue, and suitable for more amber. Each step is like 0.25 or 0.5 sometimes. Press OK to save. An asterisk shows you adjusted. To undo, center the black square.

Auto White Balance

The Auto White Balance in the D850 camera helps make colors in your photos look balanced. It looks at the colors in the picture and tries to fix them. But sometimes, colors still look different in each photo. If you only use Auto White Balance, the camera fixes the colors for each photo without remembering the previous one.

There's a setting called White Balance fine-tuning in Auto WB. It's like adjusting the colors more, but it might not be beneficial if your photos have slightly different colors. It could be helpful to take pictures in the same light for a while. However, it's a good idea to check the light's color before taking photos for the best results. The choice depends on how you like to take pictures and what you prefer.

Using Auto WB (AUTO0 to AUTO2)

You can change the colors in your photos using Auto White Balance in three ways: AUTO0 (cooler colors), AUTO1 (regular colors), and AUTO2 (warmer colors). Nikon also included a new setting, Natural Light Auto, for nature pictures. Generally, go for AUTO1 for most photos. If you want colder or warmer colors, go for AUTO0 or AUTO2. When taking pictures outside in natural light, like in the mountains, choose Natural Light Auto.

Here is how you pick the right White Balance:

- Open the Shooting Menu and pick White Balance.

- Choose Auto (or Natural Light Auto) from the list.

- If you went with Auto, select one of the three Auto WB types based on your favorite colors: AUTO0 for cooler colors, AUTO1 for normal colors, and AUTO2 for warmer colors. Press OK to confirm.

Protecting a White Balance Preset

You might have worked hard to make a specific White Balance Preset setting that you'll use a lot. Perhaps you have a studio with consistent lighting and want a reliable setting for it. Let's learn how to safeguard a Preset value (d-1 to d-6).

Here's how to do it:

1. Look at the pictures and go to the third screen.

2. Choose the setting you want to protect (like d−1 or d−6). Let's say we use d−2 as an example.

3. Press the center button on the joystick. It will open a menu.

4. Select "Protect" in the menu and move to the right.

5. Choose "On" to keep the setting safe or "Off" to remove the protection. Since we want to keep it safe, choose "On."

6. You'll see a symbol on the protected setting when you look at the screen. This symbol indicates that the setting is locked and cannot be changed. You will be able to make changes to it once you unlock it.

CHAPTER 4: CHOOSING BASIC PICTURE SETTINGS

Selecting an Exposure Mode

When using some modes on your camera, there are four ways to choose how fast the shutter opens and how much light comes in. These modes are called Program, Aperture-priority, Shutter-priority, and Manual. To switch between them, press the mode button on the top-left side of your camera and turn the main dial. Your choice depends on what kind of photo you want to take, like if you want everything to be clear or a bit blurry, if you want to capture fast movement or show motion, or if you're okay with some graininess in your picture. Each of these ways focuses on a different part of taking a picture. This part of the book will tell you about all four of them.

Aperture-Priority

In Aperture-priority mode (A), you choose how wide the camera's lens opens, and the camera automatically picks a suitable amount of time the shutter stays open to match the chosen lens opening and the ISO setting. If you change the lens opening (aperture), like going from f/5.6 to f/11, the camera will adjust the time the shutter is open to keep the picture's brightness the same. It is done using the camera's light meter.

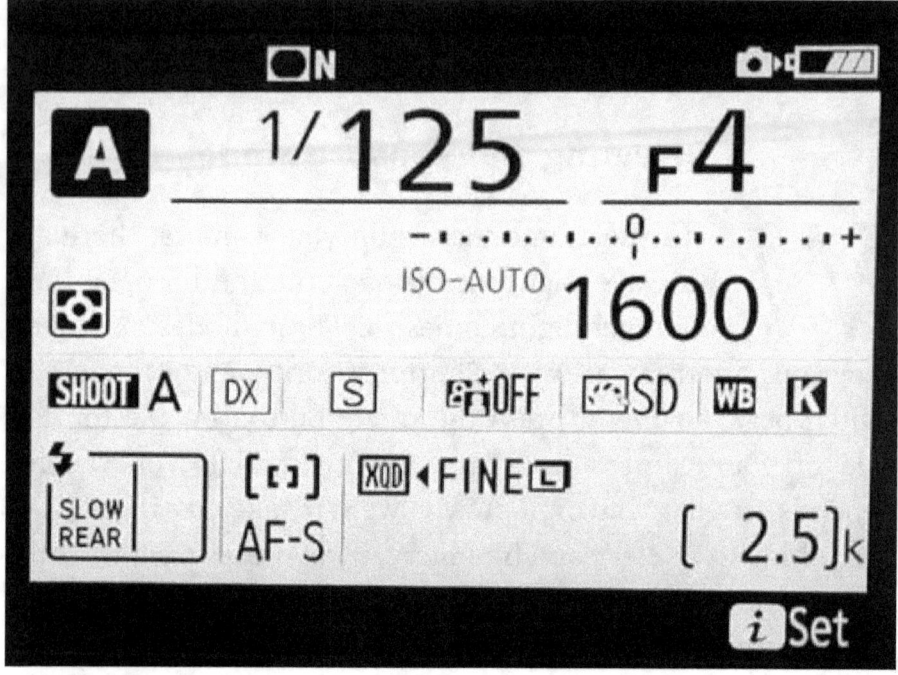

Aperture priority helps achieve a specific effect with the lens opening. For example, you might want everything in focus, so use a small f/stop like f/22 for close-up pictures. Or your main subject should be sharp and the background blurry, so you use a big f/stop. Sometimes, you might choose a certain f/stop because it gives the sharpest picture with that lens. You can also use Aperture-priority to decide a range of times the shutter should stay open, which sounds strange. For instance, if you're taking pictures of a soccer game outside with a zoomed-in lens and want fast shots, but you're okay with the time changing if clouds cover the sun, you can set the camera to A mode. You pick an aperture that makes the camera choose a shutter speed of, let's say, 1/1,000th of a second with your current ISO. Then, the camera keeps that aperture (for the right amount of focus)

but might change to 1/750th or 1/500th of a second if the light changes.

When the numbers for how quickly the camera takes a picture and the screen at the top only shows black and white flash, it means the D850 camera can't pick a good speed to take the picture when you choose the opening size for the light. It can make the picture too bright or too dark at the current camera sensitivity. It's a problem when you use "A." For instance, if you pick a small or big opening when it's sunny, the photo might still be too bright even if you use the camera's fastest speed. Or, if you choose a medium opening in a not-very-bright room, the picture might turn out blurry because the camera takes a long time to capture the image. Using "A" is better if you have some experience picking the right settings. Many experienced photographers always use "A" on their D850 cameras. The meter on the screen and viewfinder shows if the picture will be too bright or too dark.

When to use aperture-priority:

- **General landscape photography:** When taking pictures of wide outdoor views, like landscapes, the Aperture-priority mode on the D850 camera is helpful. It helps ensure that everything in your photo, from the front to the back, looks clear and sharp. If you choose a particular f/stop setting, it makes sure your whole photo is in focus.

If you pick Aperture-priority mode and set a f/stop like f/11 or f/16, you must ensure the camera's chosen shutter speed is fast enough. It is important to prevent blurriness caused by shaky hands or movement. If you're not careful, far-away leaves and tree branches might also look blurry due to movement. You can use Aperture-priority mode for the best sharpness, but you might need to increase the ISO sensitivity slightly to get a faster shutter speed. It is true whether you're holding the camera or using a tripod.

- **Specific landscape situations:** Aperture-priority mode is helpful in some specific cases, like when photographing waterfalls, and you're okay with having a long exposure time. For instance, you can set the camera to ISO 100 and a small f/stop, and the camera will choose a longer shutter speed. It will make the flowing water look smooth and blurry. Sometimes, you might need a special filter to shorten exposure time. But starting with Aperture-priority mode is a good idea.

- **Portrait photography:** Portrait photography is when you take pictures of people up close. If you want the background to be blurry, use a specific setting on your camera. Focusing on the person's face and their eyes are clear is okay if other parts are blurry. Using a medium-large opening in your camera (like f/5.6 or f/8) and a longer zoom setting (around 85mm to 135mm) will make the background behind your portrait blurry. Using a wide opening (like f/1.4), you can focus on your subject's face and blur the rest.

When you want your pictures to be very clear, different camera lenses work best in specific settings. Most lenses are clearest when the aperture is slightly closed from wide open. It makes the pictures sharp. Some lenses are even sharper when set to a slightly different aperture. For example, my 85mm f/1.4 lens is sharpest at f/2.8 or f/4. Even though it can be used wide open, it's better to be slightly closed. Similarly, my 70-200mm f/2.8 lens is best at f/4 instead of wide open. When zoomed in, a slower lens like the Nikon 28-200mm f/3.5-5.6 is the sharpest f/11. Choosing the right aperture helps you get the best results from each lens.

- **Close-up/Macro photography:** When you take close-ups or very detailed pictures, you might want parts of the picture to be blurry or clear. You can change the camera settings to control this. Sometimes, you want the subject to stand out, so you use a wider setting. Other times, you want everything to be clear, so you use a small setting. If you're taking close-up pictures and your subject isn't moving much, you can choose a specific mode on your camera to help you get the best results.

Shutter-Priority

Shutter-priority mode (S) is the opposite of Aperture-priority. You pick how fast the camera's shutter opens and closes, and then the camera decides the right amount of light to let in through the lens. If you're taking pictures of fast-moving things, you might want the shutter to capture the action quickly. Other times, you might want the shutter to be slow, so some parts of the photo look blurry, like in artsy shots. Shutter priority helps you control how much movement your camera captures.

But be careful if you use a slow shutter, like 1/8th of a second or slower. The photo could be blurry because the camera moves unless you use a special lens or have the camera on something stable like a tripod.

Like with Aperture-priority, you might run into issues if you choose a shutter speed that's too long or too short for the lighting. If that happens, the camera will let you know by blinking the shutter speed on the screen.

When to use Shutter-priority:

- To stop blurriness from subjects moving: Adjust the D850's shutter speed to a higher number to limit blurriness from moving things. The right speed depends on how fast the subject moves and how much blurriness is okay. For instance, you might use 1/1,000th of a second to capture a basketball player mid-dunk without blur or 1/200th of a second to let the wheels of a motocross racer look a bit blurry and slow motion.

- **To make a subject blur on purpose:** Sometimes, you want things to look blurry, like when photographing waterfalls, and you set the camera for a one- or two-second exposure in Shutter-priority mode.

- **To show motion blur when you're moving:** If you're following a runner with your camera, you might pick Shutter-priority mode and set it to 1/60th of a second. This way, the background blurs as you move with the runner, but the runner stays clear.

- **To prevent blur from your camera's movement:** In situations where the camera is in motion, such as shooting from a moving vehicle, shutter priority is an excellent choice to reduce blurriness caused by the camera's movement.

- **Hand-held landscape photos:** If you can't use a tripod for your landscape shots, you still want a sharp photo. Shutter priority helps by letting you set a fast enough shutter speed to avoid shaky shots. Adjust the ISO so the camera picks a good aperture for a sharp image.

- **For concerts and stage performances:** I take many pictures at concerts using my 70-200mm f/2.8 VR Nikkor lens. With the help of vibration reduction, I found that a shutter speed of 1/180th second is quick enough to prevent any shaking when I hold the D850 and this lens. It also stops most blurring caused by performers moving around, except for active ones. I chose Shutter-priority mode and set the ISO so the camera picks an aperture between f/4 and f/5.6.

Program Mode

In Program mode (P), the D850 camera chooses the correct settings, like f/stop and shutter speed, for your photo using a smart system and a database of information. If the camera can't get the correct brightness with the current settings, the shutter speed and f/stop will blink, and you can change the ISO to make the photo brighter or darker.

You can change the camera's recommended settings if you want. Use the EV (exposure value) setting to make the photo brighter or darker than the camera suggests. Also, in Program mode, you can turn a dial to use different settings that still give the same brightness but with different f/stop and shutter speed combinations.

It is called the "Flexible Program" by Nikon. Turn the main dial left to make the aperture smaller (like changing from f/4 to f/5.6). It will make the camera use a slower shutter speed (like going from 1/200th to 1/125th second). Turn the main dial right to use a larger aperture, and the camera will automatically set a faster shutter speed to keep the exposure the same as in the normal mode. When you've changed the settings, you'll see an asterisk near the "P" on the screen. Your changes will stay until you turn the dial back or switch to a different mode.

When to use Program mode:

- **When you are rushing to get a shot:** The D850 camera will determine the correct exposure for you without your input when you want to take a quick photo.

- **When you give the camera to someone new:** Set the D850 to P mode, hand the camera to a friend or someone you trust, show them where the buttons are, and tell them to look through the viewfinder and press the button to take a picture.

- **When you don't need specific settings for motion or focus:** If your subject doesn't need special techniques to avoid blurriness or create specific effects, and you don't need to control how much is in focus or blurry, you can use P mode as a general option. You can still change some settings easily if you want to control the focus or motion in the photo.

Manual Exposure

Being a skilled photographer involves understanding when to utilize your D850's automation through the P mode and when to opt for semi-automatic modes like S or A. When to manually adjust the exposure using M. Some photographers prefer manual exposure settings, as the D850 can provide indications when its metering system deems the manual adjustments offer the correct exposure, using the analog exposure scale at the viewfinder's bottom.

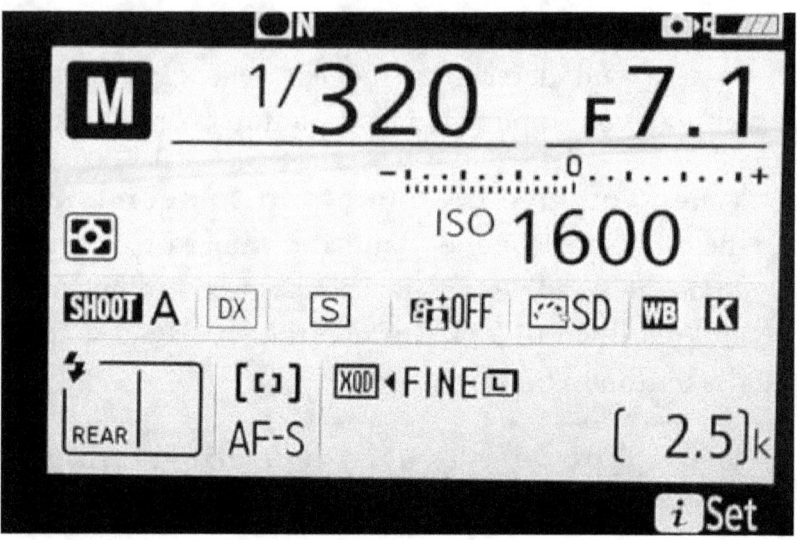

Manual exposure proves helpful in some scenarios. For instance, capturing a silhouette photo might require precise control that neither exposure modes nor EV correction can achieve. Setting the exposure manually allows you to precisely tailor the shutter speed and f-stop. Similarly, when working in a studio with multiple flash units triggered by slave devices, the camera's exposure meter won't account for extra illumination. In such cases, manual aperture adjustments are necessary.

Depending on what you like, you might only have to adjust how bright or dark the picture is, sometimes manually. Understanding how it works is still very important. Luckily, the D850 camera makes it easy to adjust these settings manually. Just follow these steps: change the mode to Manual, set the shutter speed using one dial, and adjust the aperture using another dial. After that, the camera will show you if your settings match the correct exposure.

Here's when you should use Manual exposure:

- **When working in the studio:** You should use Manual mode when you're in a studio because you have full control over the lighting. The camera won't try to change things on its own. In Manual mode, you can decide how bright the picture is by choosing the shutter speed, aperture, and ISO settings.

- **When using non-dedicated flash:** When you use certain types of camera flashes, There are systems like Nikon Creative Lighting System (CLS) and Advanced Lighting System (ALS) that work well with cameras like D850. They can help you control external flashes like SB-5000 or SB-910. However, the camera must know how strong the flash is if you use different flashes, like studio ones connected through the D850's PC/X connector. So, you'll need to adjust the aperture setting manually.

- **If you have a handheld light meter:** You can figure out the right aperture for flash photos and pictures taken with continuous lighting using a handheld light meter. This meter can measure both kinds of light and tell you the best aperture. It's helpful because you can measure different parts of the scene separately and adjust your camera settings in Manual mode.

- **When you plan on outsmarting a metering system:** When you want to do something creative with exposure, The camera's automatic metering system is good at dealing with tricky lighting, like bright backlighting or dark shadows. You may want to do something different sometimes. With Manual exposure, you can intentionally make silhouettes, create a bright and glowing look by overexposing, or make things moody and dark by underexposing. It enables you to get more control over your photos.

Choosing a Release Mode

The shooting mode decides when and how the D850 takes a picture. If you're coming from a point-and-shoot camera, you might be familiar with the term "drive modes," which used to be called that in the film camera days. These options included single-shot or continuous shooting modes. The D850 has seven ways to take a photo: Single shot, Slow continuous, Fast continuous, Quiet shot, Quiet continuous, Self-timer, and Mirror Up.

Here's what these modes mean:

- **Single frame:** When you use this mode, the D850 takes one photo each time you press the shutter button down. If you press the shutter and nothing happens, it might be because your camera is set to focus first before taking a photo. This is called focus priority, and you can learn more about it in the section about "Choosing a Focus Mode."

- **Continuous low speed (CL) mode:** Continuous low speed (CL) mode is like taking pictures slowly, but it can also be a bit faster. You can choose to take 1 to 6 pictures per second or 1 to 8 pictures per second if you use a special battery setup. You can adjust this in the camera settings. I use this mode when I don't need many fast pictures, like when taking multiple shots at once or when the scene isn't changing quickly.

- **Continuous high speed (CH):** Continuous high speed (CH) mode takes pictures quickly, up to 7 frames per second (or 9 frames with the grip and special battery). The speed can get slower when your D850's memory starts to get full. The camera needs to wait until the photos you've taken are saved to the memory card so it has space to take more. The speed can also go down if you use certain settings or conditions, like slow shutter speeds, high ISO, small apertures, or when some other things are happening with the camera.

- **Silent Shutter Release:** When you turn on this mode with the Q symbol, the D850 camera becomes quieter. It turns off the beeping sound, makes the flipping mirror quieter, and delays the noise until you let go of the shutter button.

- **Continuous Silent Shutter Release:** With this mode, the D850 takes pictures continuously at a speed of up to 3 frames per second, but the noise it makes is a bit quieter than usual.

Setting Resolution and File Type (The Image Quality Setting)

Changing the Image Quality Setting

Image quality refers to the kind of picture your camera produces. Your D850 camera can take pictures like NEF/RAW, JPEG, JPEG images, and TIFF.

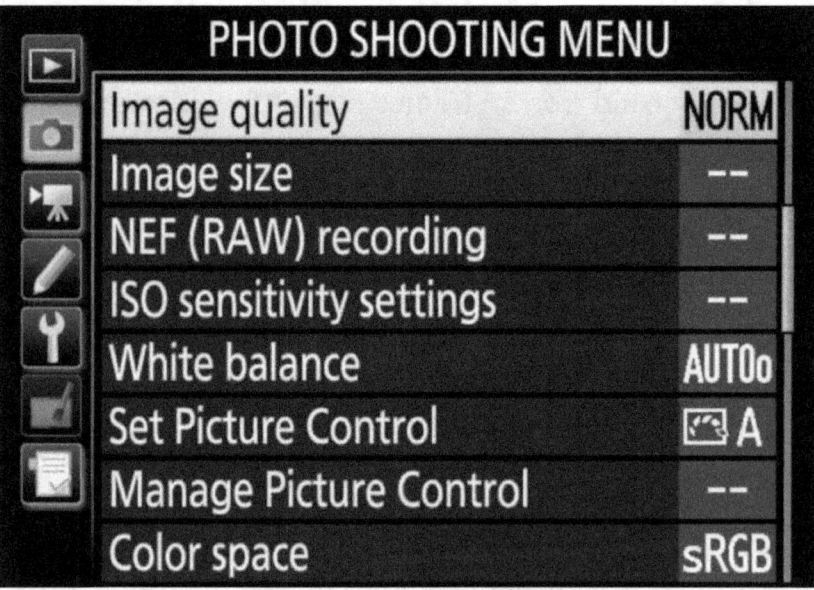

I'll look at each type closely and discuss the good and not-so-good things about them. By the time we're done, you'll know more about these types and can pick the best one for the kind of pictures you're taking. Here's how you can choose the image quality setting:

Setting the Image Quality With the Menu System

To pick the image quality, follow these steps using the Menu:

1. Go to the Photo Shooting Menu and choose Image quality, then move to the right.

2. Pick one of the 14 Image quality options and press OK to select it.

Setting Image Quality with External Camera Controls

You can also use the QUAL button, the dial on the back, the Control panel, or the Information display to change the image quality. This way is quicker than using the menus.

Here's how to change the image quality using the camera's external controls:

1. Press and hold the QUAL button.

2. Turn the back dial to pick the Image quality (like RAW, TIFF, FINE, NORM, or BASIC). FINE, NORM, and BASIC are for different levels of JPEG quality, with varying compression. I picked FINEimage (the best quality JPEG fine) displayed on the Control panel and Information display. You can access the Information display in image 4 along with the other controls by pressing the info button.

3. When you've chosen a quality, let go of the QUAL button to confirm the changes.

Considering resolution: Large, Medium, or Small?

The image size setting on your camera determines how many megapixels your photos will have. By default, the D850 camera's image size is set to "Large" which has 45.4 megapixels for JPEG, RAW, and TIFF files. You can change this megapixel rating by choosing from five different image area sizes (like full-frame, cropped, etc.). This choice only affects the size of the image in megapixels. The steps to set the image size for JPEG and TIFF files are provided, and it's important to note that the pixel ratio and megapixel size will change depending on the chosen image area setting.

Image Size for JPEG/TIFF Files

Here are the screens and steps to choose the Image size for JPEG and TIFF pictures. Both types have the same number of megapixels, but their file sizes (how much space they take up) will differ. JPEG pictures are squished to save space, while TIFF pictures aren't squished and take up more space. Both types have 8 colors in each pixel.

Keep in mind: the size of the picture in pixels (like 8256 × 5504) and the megapixels (like 45.4 M) will change based on the Image area you picked earlier (like FX, 1.2x, DX, 5:4, 1:1), which we talked about a few pages ago. The numbers you see here are for the FX Image area. If you switch to a different Image area, these Image size numbers will change, too.

Image Size for NEF (RAW) Files

The D850 camera offers three NEF (RAW) Image sizes to give you more choices than older Nikon cameras. You can choose between Large (L), Medium (M), and Small (S) for RAW images.

The values for Image size change depending on the Image area you picked before (like FX, 1.2x, DX, 5:4, 1:1). In this part, we'll focus on the values for the FX Image area.

Setting the Image Size Using External Camera Controls

Here's how to quickly change the Image size without using the regular menu. You can also do this using the camera's physical controls.

Here's how:

1. Hold down the QUALITY (QUAL) button.

2. Turn the front dial to select your desired image size (Large, Medium, or Small).

3. You'll see the image size change on the Control Panel or Information display. You can press the info button to see this display.

4. Let go of the QUALITY button to confirm the new image size.

Understanding file type

If you're new to using a DSLR camera, you might not be sure which picture format to use. It's a good idea to use all three formats at different times. Let's quickly talk about these formats:

1. **NEF (RAW):** This format is for photographers who like to edit their pictures on a computer. When you take a picture in RAW, the camera saves all the light information without making the picture look good right away. You need to work on it later on your computer to make it look great. This takes more effort, but the pictures can be high quality. The camera even has a feature that lets you change RAW pictures to regular JPEG ones. The files' size can differ depending on how you save them. For example, when I took a picture of leaves on the ground, the file sizes were 62.5 MB for the best quality, 53.2 MB for slightly lower quality, and 98.5 MB for the biggest size.

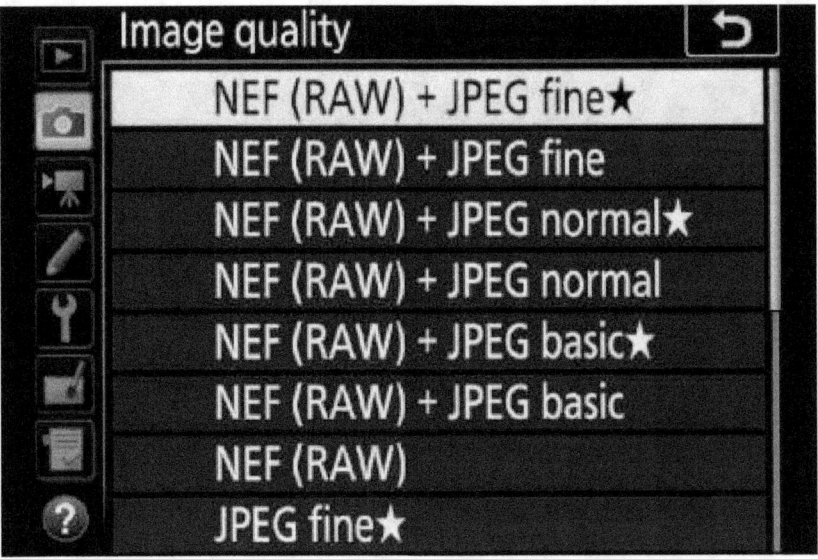

2. **JPEG:** JPEG is an image format that's quick to use. It's good for when you want to use a picture right away. But, it throws away some picture details to make the file smaller. The picture that's left still looks nice, but you can't change it a lot without it getting worse. If you need to work with pictures later, it's better to use another format. JPEG files are smaller than some other types, like NEF, and can be different sizes based on how complex the picture is. The camera has different settings for making JPEG files with more or less detail. Pictures with a star symbol have the best quality, and pictures without a star are smaller but not as good. For example, when I took a picture of leaves on the ground, the file sizes were different based on the settings I used.

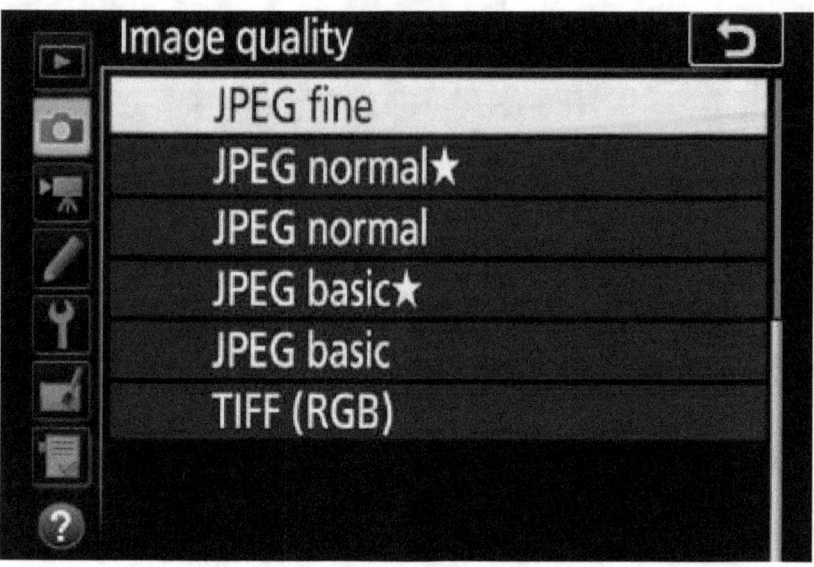

3. **TIFF (RGB):** The 8-bit TIFF file that comes from the camera is similar to a JPEG, but it doesn't compress the image. You can use this image without changing it. The camera's 12- to 14-bit RAW file, which holds more detail, gets turned into an 8-bit TIFF, losing some data. So, initially, TIFF is a bit lossy, giving up some image quality. But once you have the TIFF file, you can make changes and save it without losing more quality. If you need a file for immediate use and want to make changes to it, and you're not familiar with RAW files, TIFF is a good choice. The downside is that TIFF files are quite large. For example, a picture of fall leaves became a TIFF file of 143.6 MB. Having a lot of these can fill up your memory cards quickly.

CHAPTER 5: CAPTURING VIDEOS

Viewing Your Movies

After you're done recording your movies, you can watch and review them. When you're reviewing the pictures, the movie clips will appear, just like regular photos. But you can tell they're videos because they have a movie camera symbol and a "Play" message on them. To start watching, press the middle button on the multi-selector.

While the video is playing, you can do a few things:

- **Pause:** To stop the video temporarily, press the downward button on the multi-selector. Press the middle button to start playing again.

- **Rewind/Advance:** If you want to go back or forward in the video, use the left or right buttons on the multi-selector. If you press once, it's like 2 times the speed of normal. Press twice for 8 times the speed, and three times for 16 times the speed. If you hold the left or right buttons, you can go to the very beginning or the end of the video.

- **Slow Motion:** If you want to see the video in slow motion, press the downward button while the video is paused.

- **Skip 10 Seconds:** Turn the main dial to jump 10 seconds ahead or back.

- **Skip to Index:** Turn the small dial to move to the next or previous index point in the video. If there aren't any index points, the dial will take you to the last or first frame of the video. Videos with index points have a special icon at the top of the screen.

- **Change Volume:** Use the Zoom In and Zoom Out buttons to make the sound louder or quieter.

- **Edit or Save Frame:** If you want to edit the video or save a single frame, press the "i" button and follow the steps in the next section.

- **Exit Playback:** To stop watching the video, press the upward button on the multi-selector or the Playback button.

- **Go Back to Recording:** If you want to start recording again, press the shutter release button.

- **Access Menus:** If you need to use the menus while watching, press the MENU button.

Trimming Your Movies

Editing videos directly in the camera is only possible for cutting the beginning or end of a clip, and the clip must be at least two seconds long. For more advanced editing, you'll need a special program that can edit a type of video called AVI. You can find these programs by searching "AVI Editor" online. There are many free options available, or you can use paid programs like

Corel Video Studio, Adobe Premiere Elements, or Pinnacle Studio. These programs let you put together multiple clips into one video, add titles, cool effects, and smooth transitions between scenes.

If you want to do the basic editing right in the camera, you can do it from the Retouch menu or while watching the video playback. Here's how you do it:

1. **Start Watching:** Use the Playback button to start checking your pictures, and when you see a video clip you want to edit, press the middle button on the multi-selector to start watching it. If you want, you can also go to the Retouch menu and pick "Edit Movie" when looking at the clip.

2. **Begin the Edit:** To remove parts from the start of the clip, watch the video until you see the first part you want to keep. Then, press the down button to pause. You can move back and forth frame by frame while the video is paused using the left and right buttons or turning the main or sub-command dials.

3. **Trim the End:** If you want to cut something from the end of the clip, watch until you reach the last part you want to keep, and then press the down button to pause. If you've set any specific points in the video, you can jump to them by turning the main dial.

4. **Pick Where to Edit:** While the video is paused, press the "i" button to see editing options, and choose "Choose

69

Start/End Point." You'll be asked if the current frame should be the starting or ending point. Choose your preference and press OK.

5. **Continue Watching:** Press the middle button to continue playing the video. You can use the pause, rewind, advance, single-frame controls, and the main dial (to jump to set points), as mentioned earlier, to move around in the clip. Remember, your trimmed video has to be at least two seconds long.

6. **Confirm the Edit:** A message will pop up asking if you want to proceed. Select Yes or No and press OK.

7. **Save the Edited Video:** You have four choices for saving the trimmed video:

   • **Save as New File:** The edited clip will be saved as a new file, and the original video will stay as it is.

   • **Overwrite Existing File:** The edited clip will replace the original on your memory card. Be careful, as you won't be able to get the unedited version back.

   • **Cancel:** Go back to the editing mode.

   • **Preview:** Watch the trimmed version. Then you can decide to save it as a new file, overwrite the original, or cancel.

When you save the trimmed clip, the camera will show a message and a progress bar while it's saving. This takes some time, so don't stop it midway. Make sure your camera battery is fully charged before you start editing to avoid any issues.

Saving a Frame

You can keep a picture from your video as a regular picture, like a photo. Here's how:

1. While you're watching your video, pause it on the part you want to keep. Just press the down button to stop it.

2. Press the "i" button and pick "Save Selected Frame".

3. Press the up button to actually save the picture you picked.

4. Choose "Proceed" and press OK to say "Yes, save it!"

5. The picture will be saved on your memory card, and you'll see a little scissors icon on it.

Movie Shooting Menus

The Movie Shooting Menu is like a special menu, just like the Photo Shooting Menu we talked about before. But this menu is for making videos instead of photos. It has settings specifically for creating videos.

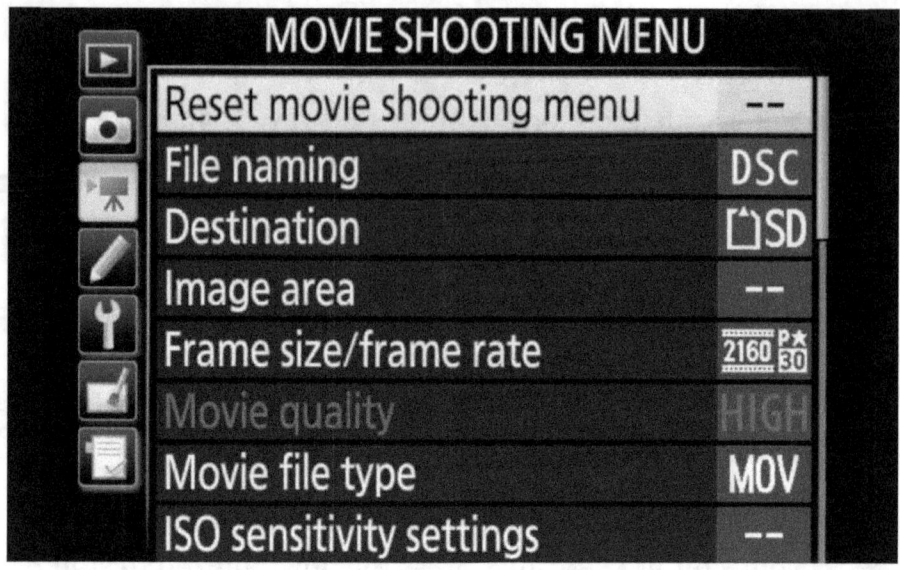

In older Nikon cameras, finding the video settings was a bit tricky because they were mixed with the picture settings. But now, Nikon has made a separate menu just for video settings. This makes it much easier to set up your camera for good-quality videos.

Reset movie shooting menu

The "Reset movie shooting menu" option does exactly what it sounds like. It takes all the settings in the Movie Shooting Menu and returns them to how they were when the camera was brand new. If you want to begin again with the original settings, you can use this function.

File naming

The File naming function lets you change the first three letters in a video's name to something you like. By default, it's "DSC." You could use your initials, numbers, letters, or a mix.

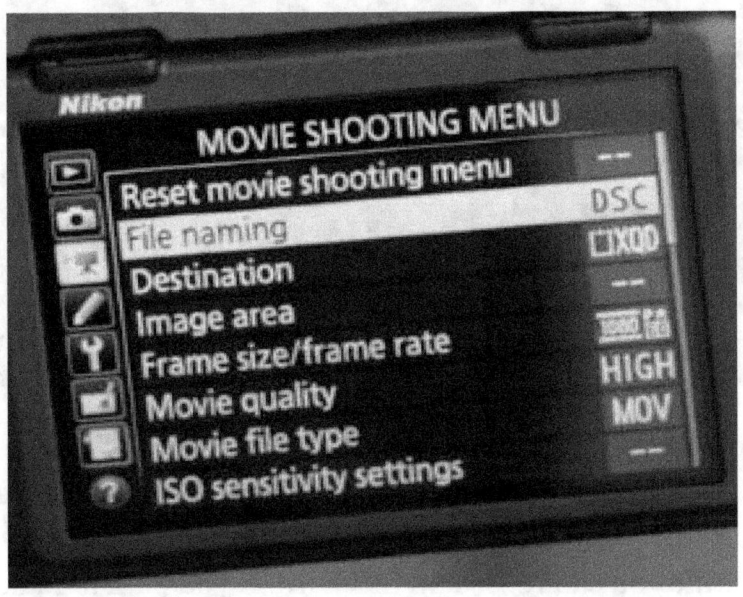

It works like the File naming function in the Photo Shooting Menu I discussed earlier. In that section, there's a suggestion to keep track of the number of photos you've taken. This helps when your camera changes the file name from DSC-9999 to DSC-0001 after 9999 photos.

But if you're not using your D850 mostly for making videos, you might not worry much about going past 9999 videos. If you are worried, you can keep track of when your camera's videos go from 9999 to 0001.

Destination

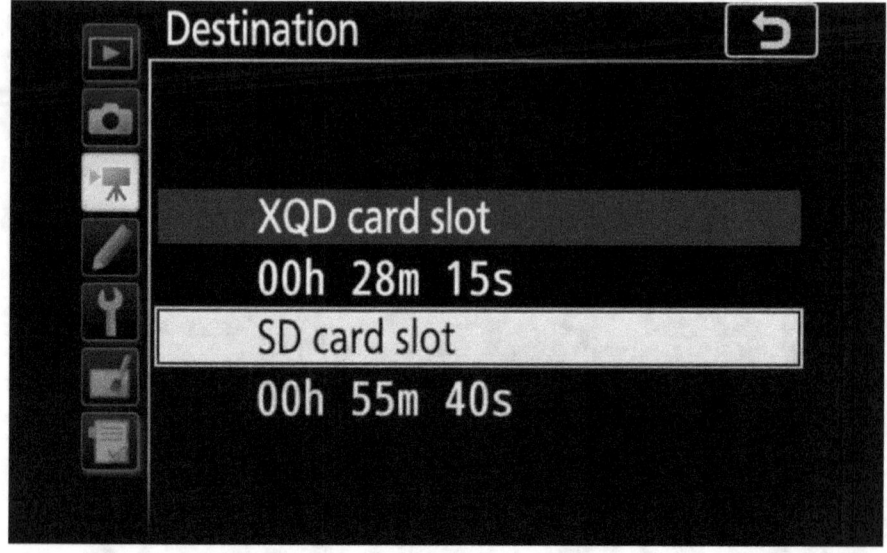

Destination helps you pick which memory card will save your videos. Under the card options, you'll see something like 03h 18m 28s (h=hours, m=minutes, s=seconds). This shows how much time you can record on that card. If you plan to make lots of videos, it's smart to get big memory cards – you'll need them!

Image area

The Image area function is there to help you. It lets you use the regular view for most videos, and when you need to get closer to far-away or small things, you can use the DX crop mode.

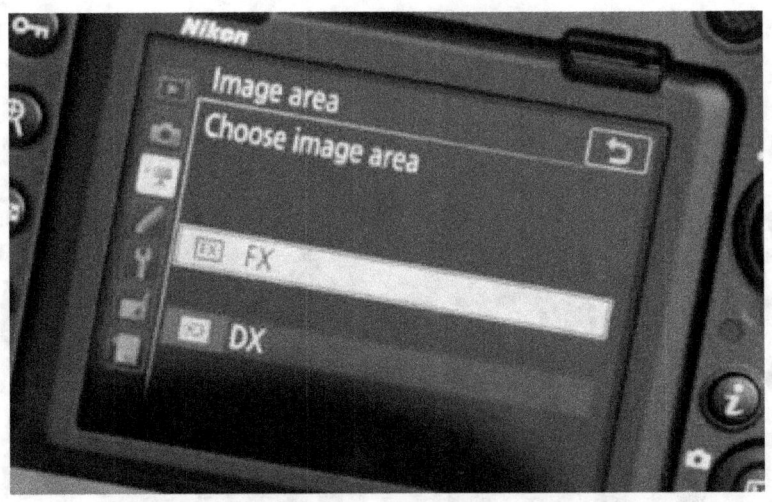

When you pick either of these modes, the camera will adjust the picture size to fit the screen where you're seeing the live view. Unlike in the viewfinder where you see a grayed-out box when using DX mode for photos, there's no such thing here. The camera shows you exactly what the video will capture.

This is easier when making a video because you don't need to worry about keeping things within lines on the screen. The video just fits the screen and shows only what the camera is recording.

Movie quality

Movie quality affects how quickly the camera records videos. It's like how the type of JPEG (Fine, Normal, Basic) affects photo quality. A higher bit rate means better video quality. There are two-bit rates for videos saved on the memory card:

High quality and Normal. The Frame size and frame rate of the video decide which one is used.

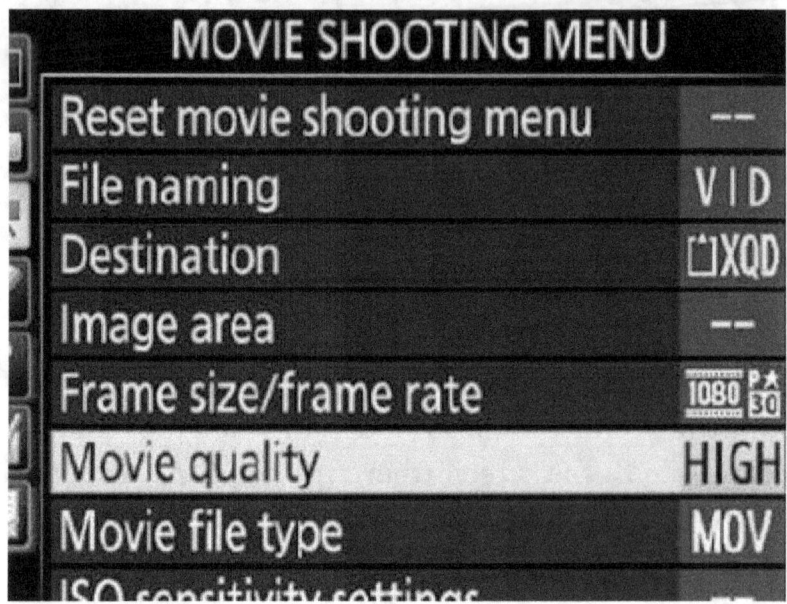

If you can't choose Movie quality in the menu, it might be because you're using one of the three 4K UHD (2160p) video modes. In those modes, the camera always uses High quality.

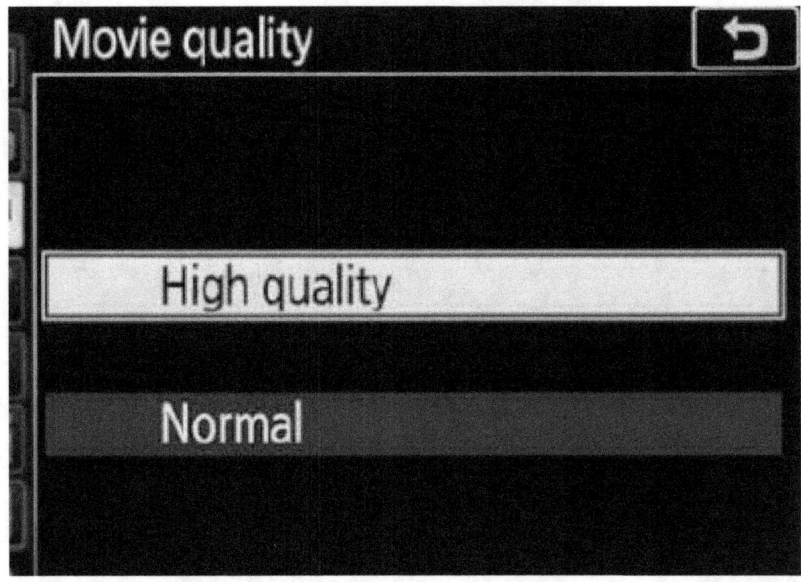

Movie file type

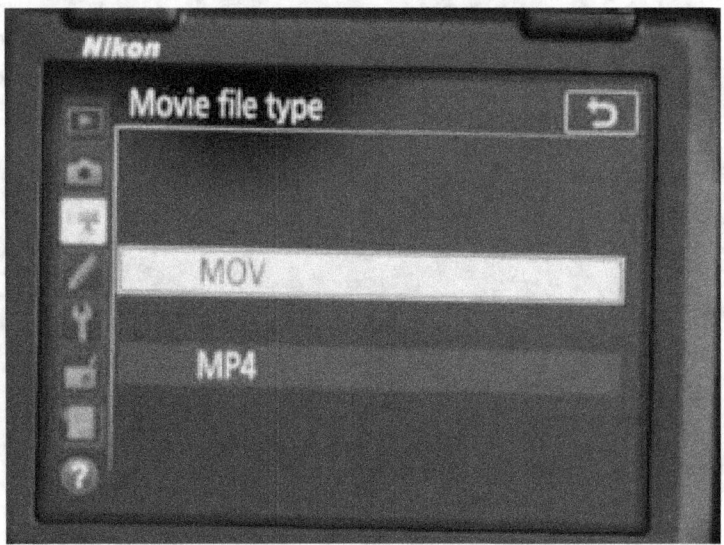

The D850 camera usually saves videos in a format called MOV, which works with Apple QuickTime. But you can also pick MP4, which is good for internet streaming and works well on computers and smart devices. Both MOV and MP4 will play on most movie apps.

ISO sensitivity settings

Movie ISO sensitivity settings let you control how sensitive the camera's sensor is to light while you're making a video. You can decide to control it yourself or let the camera do it automatically.

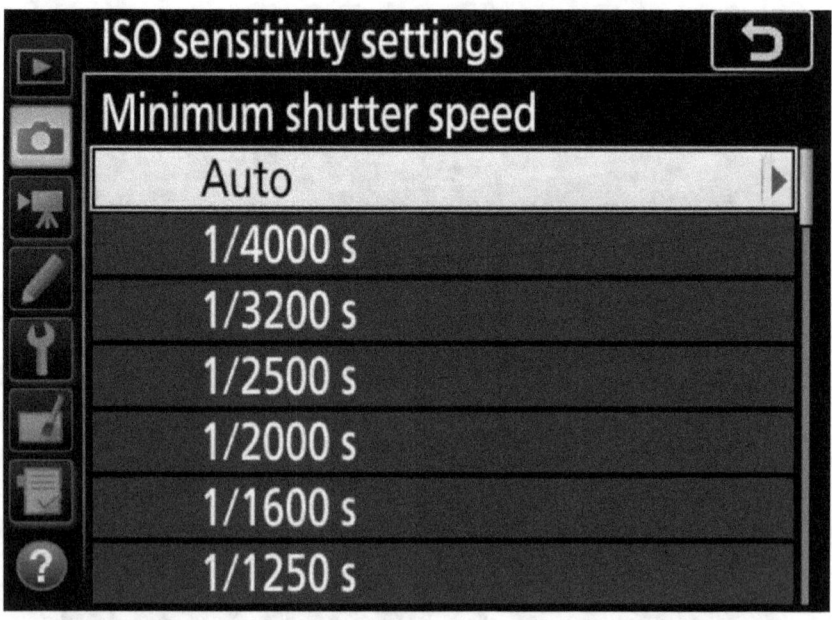

Because light can change when you move the camera around, it's usually a good idea to let the D850 adjust the ISO automatically. If you don't, your video could end up too dark or too bright. Sometimes you might set a specific ISO, like when you're in a place with steady lighting. But in general, it's better to let the camera change the ISO as needed. This way, you can focus on making the best video shots.

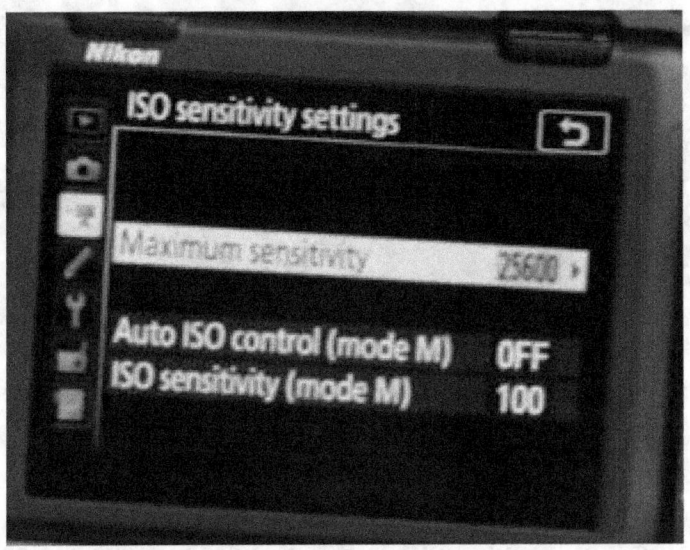

White balance

Setting the White balance (WB) for videos is a lot like what you do for photos. You can pick a specific type of WB like Sunlight, Fluorescent, or Cloudy. Or you can let the camera decide using Auto WB.

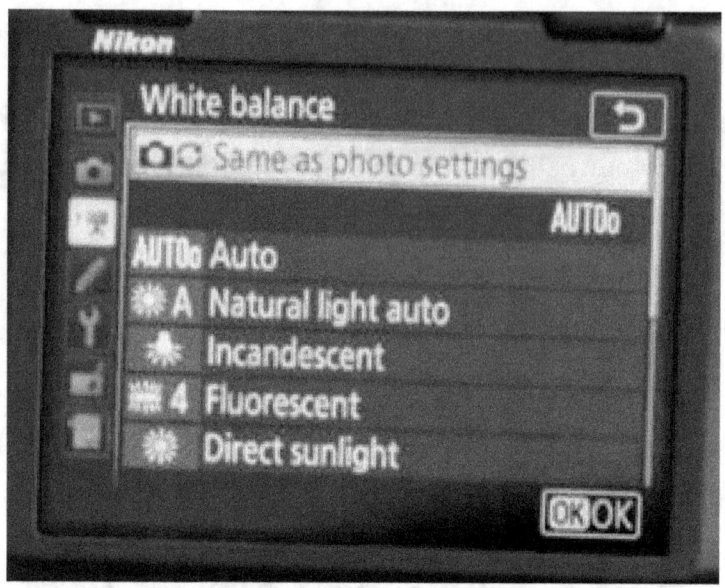

If you want accurate colors, you can choose a color temperature from 2500K to 10000K. You can also use a white or gray card to measure the light around and match the colors best.

Everything you know about WB for photos works the same for videos. In this section, we'll focus on picking the right WB. For more about using White balance, you can check out other parts.

Set Picture Control

The "Set Picture Control" tool lets you pick from eight Nikon Picture Controls to give your video a certain style. It works the same for both videos and photos. The default setting is the same as what you used last time for photos.

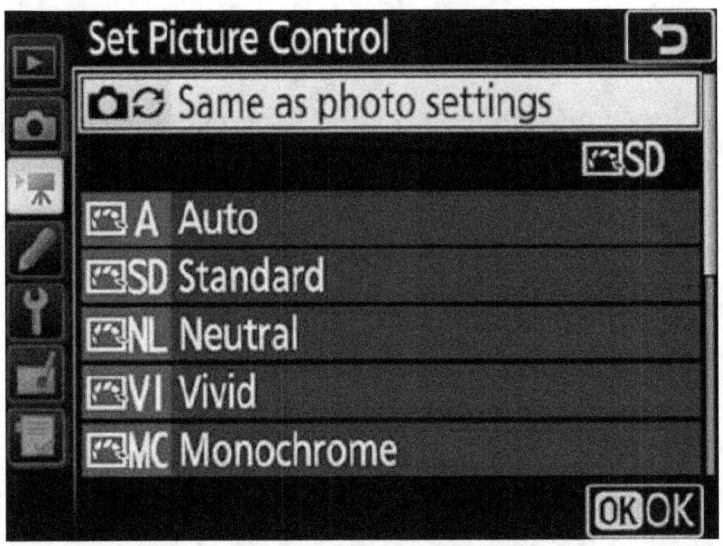

Each Picture Control has its settings for things like sharpness, clarity, contrast, brightness, color strength, and color tone. There's also a Quick adjust that quickly changes sharpness, contrast, and color together.

Here are the options on the Set Picture Control menu and what each does for your videos:

- **Same as photo settings:** Uses the same settings as your last photos (default).

- **A Auto:** The Portrait/Landscape Picture Control starts with the Standard one, but it's adjusted for portraits and landscapes. When the camera sees a person's face, it makes their skin tones softer and nicer. For landscapes, it makes the greenery and sky a bit more colorful (not as much as the Vivid setting). Everything else looks like the Standard Picture Control.

81

- **SD Standard:** This setting makes your videos look balanced regarding sharpness, contrast, brightness, colors, and shades. It's good for most videos and doesn't make colors too strong or too weak.

- **NL Neutral:** This setting gives your videos a softer look with less sharpness, contrast, brightness, colors, and shades. It's good for videos where you want less intense colors and contrast.

- **VI Vivid:** This setting makes your videos look vibrant with strong sharpness, contrast, brightness, colors, and shades. It's best for nature videos where you want bold reds, blues, and greens. Avoid using it for videos with important skin tones, which might make colors and contrast too strong.

- **MC Monochrome:** This Picture Control is for people who enjoy making videos with a classic black-and-white style. The regular settings in this control are average, so you might want to try different contrast settings. It also has filter effects that work, like putting on a colored filter (yellow, orange, red, green) for special looks. Plus, you can add tones to change the video's color in cool ways. You get choices like B&W, sepia, cyanotype, and different colors.

- **PT Portrait:** This Picture Control is great for videos with people, especially when you want their skin tones to look good. It's a bit more colorful and has more contrast than the NL Neutral control. But it's not as strong as the SD Standard control and nowhere near as colorful as the VI Vivid control.

- **LS Landscape:** This Picture Control is for folks who want natural-looking landscape videos without the extra color boost of the VI Vivid control. It does make colors a bit more vibrant, but they won't be too intense.

- **FL Flat:** This Picture Control is for professional video makers. It makes videos with low sharpness, contrast, and color. This gives the most range between light and dark (low contrast) and less colorful shots. Professionals can later adjust colors, sharpness, and contrast using video editing software.

If you keep this function as "Same as photo settings," the camera uses the same Picture Control for photos and videos. But if you choose a specific Picture Control, it separates the settings for photos and videos. Each gets its settings.

Here's how you can choose a Picture Control for your videos:

1. Go to the Movie Shooting Menu and choose Set Picture Control. Then scroll to the right.

2. If you want the same settings for photos and videos, pick "Same as photo settings." This way, your video settings will match your photo settings. Press OK to confirm and skip the next steps.

3. If you want different settings for photos and videos, scroll down and choose one of the eight Picture Controls. Press OK unless you want to adjust its settings. If you do, scroll right.

4. Change Sharpening, Contrast, Brightness, Saturation, and Hue for each Picture Control. Some controls don't have Quick Adjust for video. And none of them use Clarity for video. To change things, scroll up or down to pick a setting. Then, scroll left (-) or right (+) to adjust it. Each setting's name explains what it does. If you change a Picture Control, you'll see a little star next to it in the menus. That means it's changed. When you're done, press OK to save. Press the Delete button to reset a Picture Control's settings and choose Yes. It'll ask if you're sure, and you press OK if you are.

Active D-Lighting

The Active D-Lighting tool helps you adjust the contrast when recording videos. If the shadows are too dark, you can make them brighter to see more details. And if the bright parts are almost turning pure white, you can make them a bit darker to keep the details in those bright areas.

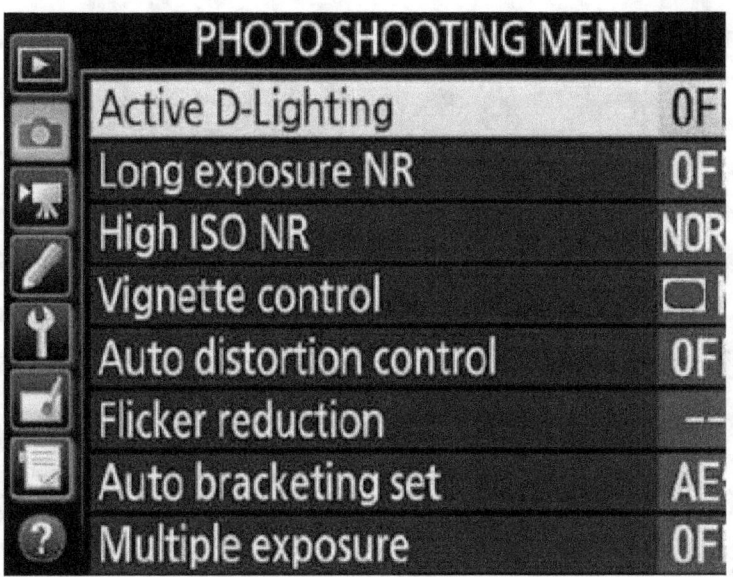

High ISO NR

High ISO NR (High ISO Noise Reduction) helps reduce the grainy look in your videos when you use high ISO settings.

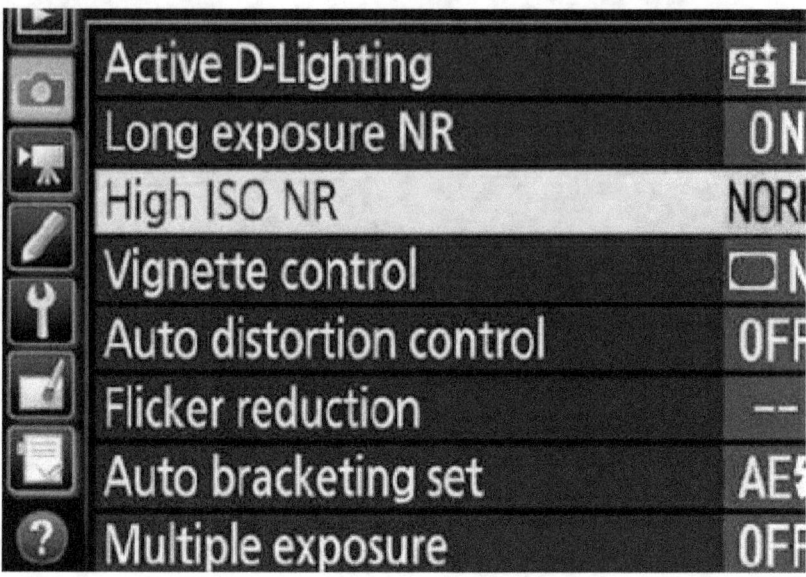

The D850 camera handles noise better than many others. It can shoot videos at ISO 3200 with little noise. But all cameras have some noise, so it's smart to reduce it when using high ISO.

Even if the High ISO NR is off, the camera does a little noise reduction, just not as much as the Low setting. So, when you use high ISO, there's still some noise reduction happening.

You can choose how much noise reduction you want with four settings: High, Normal, Low, or Off.

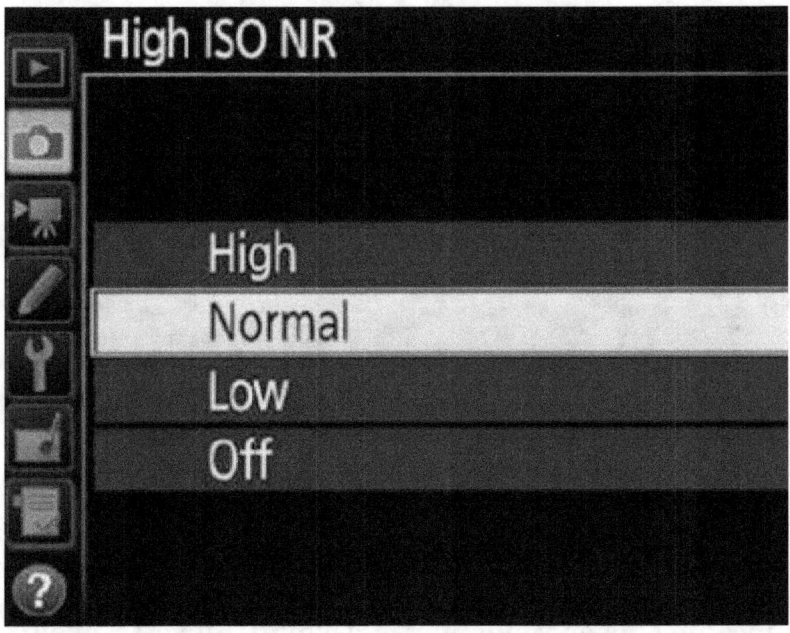

Flicker reduction

Flicker reduction helps prevent that dark band that moves down the video screen, making it look odd. It happens when you record under certain lights, like fluorescent or mercury-vapor ones.

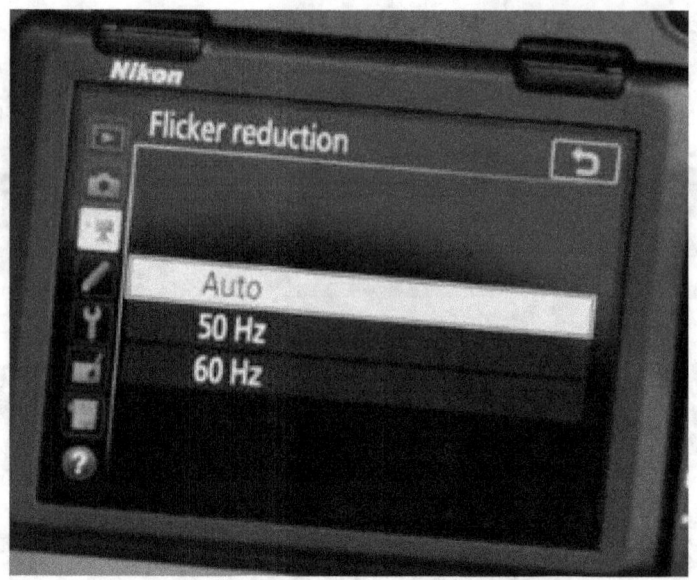

Turning on Flicker reduction is a smart move to avoid this issue. You can start with Auto Flicker reduction. It makes the camera adjust how it takes frames to reduce the banding.

If Auto doesn't work well, you can pick a 50Hz- or 60Hz settings. Choose the one that works best.

Sometimes, when things are really bright, the flicker can be worse. Using a smaller aperture like f/8 or smaller can help in that case.

Attenuator

The Attenuator is like a helper that changes how sensitive the microphone is to loud sounds. Imagine you're recording a sports event; the crowd gets really loud when someone scores.

The Attenuator makes the microphone less sensitive so that the loud noise doesn't make the recording too noisy.

Frequency response

The Frequency response function lets you choose how audio sounds when recording a video. Sound is important for good videos!

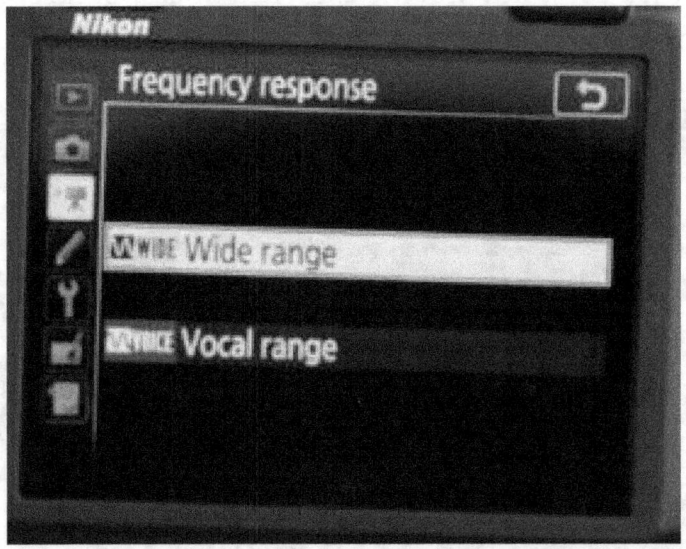

Imagine you're filming in the jungle and want to hear all the birds chirping, leaves rustling, and bugs buzzing. Or, you might be filming a speaker and want to avoid hearing people walking or birds outside.

The Nikon D850 helps you control sound quality better than older models. Using Microphone sensitivity, Attenuator, and Frequency response together can give you great sound.

Microphone sensitivity decides how well the mic hears; the Attenuator stops loud sounds from messing up, and Frequency response picks which sound tones the mic catches. We've talked about the first two, now let's see what Frequency response does.

Wind noise reduction

The Wind noise reduction tool helps get rid of that annoying sound when the wind hits the camera's microphone spots. But it doesn't work with extra mics on the camera's accessory shoe.

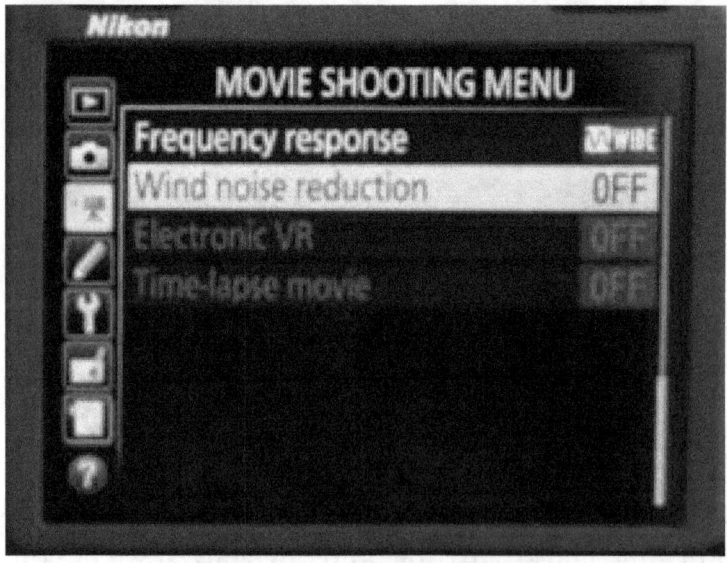

Have you ever recorded a video on a windy day and heard that annoying rumble instead of clear sound later?

While you might not fully get rid of it without special mics, you can lessen it with a special filter. This filter blocks low sounds like wind rumbles.

Good news for D850 users: there's a filter you can turn on when recording videos outside. It helps cut down wind noise.

But remember, if you're recording music with deep, low sounds like cellos and bass, the filter might cut some of the depth. So, it's not a good idea to always leave it on. Let's learn how to turn Wind noise reduction on and off.

Electronic VR

The Electronic VR helps you steady your videos when you shoot without a tripod. Unlike some cameras, it doesn't move the sensor physically. Instead, it slightly shifts the video frame to make it more stable.

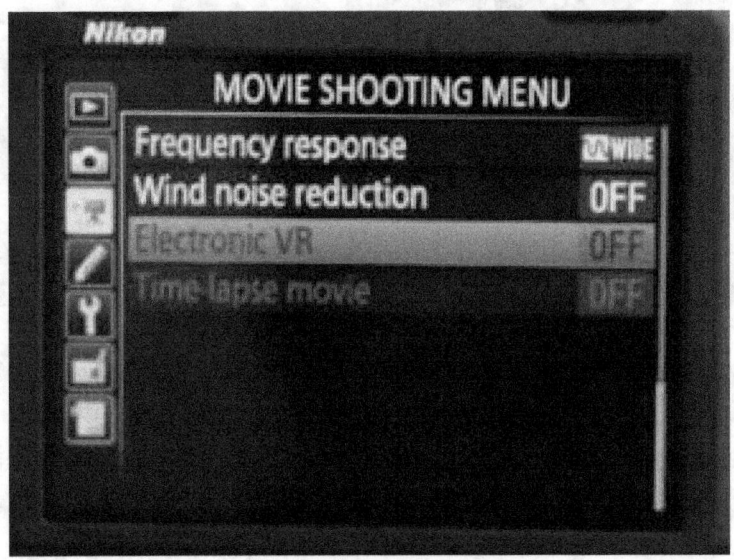

When you're holding the camera while shooting, tiny shakes happen. The camera tries to shift the pixels capturing the video to match those shakes.

Electronic VR works with the regular VR in Nikkor lenses to make your video steadier.

Time-lapse movie

A time-lapse movie is like a close relative of interval timer shooting. The main difference is that a time-lapse movie makes a quiet video showing changes over time. When you make a time-lapse movie, the camera takes pictures at specific times that you choose and then puts them together into a video.

CONCLUSION

The Nikon D850 is a powerful and versatile DSLR camera that offers a wide range of features and capabilities for photographers of all levels. With its 45.7-megapixel full-frame sensor, EXPEED 5 image processor, and 153-point autofocus system, the D850 can produce stunning images in various conditions.

The D850 is also well-suited for video recording, offering 4K UHD video at 30fps or Full HD video at 120fps. The camera also features a tilting touchscreen display, built-in Wi-Fi and Bluetooth, and a weather-sealed body.

In this user guide, I have covered the basics of using the Nikon D850, from setting up the camera to taking your first photos. I have also discussed some of the camera's more advanced features, such as autofocus, metering, and white balance.

I hope that this guide has helped you to get started with your Nikon D850. With a little practice, you can take stunning photos and videos with this amazing camera.